Blow-Drying a Chicken

Observations from a Working Poet

D0730951

Poets notice what other people miss.
Nationally-known poet Molly Fisk's singular
perspective on love, death, grammar, lingerie,
small towns, and the natural world
will get you laughing, crying, and thinking.

Blow-Drying a Chicken

Observations from a Working Poet

Molly Fisk

Story Street Press
Nevada City, California
2013

Published by Story Street Press
10068 Newtown Rd.
Nevada City, CA 95959
e-mail: molly@mollyfisk.com
www.mollyfisk.com

This edition was produced for on-demand distribution by
lightningsource.com for Story Street Press.

Cover design: Maxima Kahn
Proofreading: Judy Crowe
Typesetting: Wordsworth (wordsworthofmarin.com)
Author photo: Alan Pomatto
Editorial Support: Marilyn Kriegel, Judie Rae
Technical Support: Nancy Shanteau, Paul Emery, Steve
Baker, Catherine Stifter
Original inspiration: Carolyn Crane
Frequency: KVMR 89.5 FM Nevada City, CA, kvmr.org

The individual essays in this book originally aired as commentary on the News Hour of community radio station KVMR in
Nevada City, CA between 2004 and 2013 (© Molly Fisk). Download recent commentary for public radio airplay in a strict 4-minute format by contacting Creative PR at info@creativepr.org for
the FTP link. There is no charge. This material is brought to you
by the author and by KVMR 89.5 FM Nevada City, California
through a grant from the Corporation for Public Broadcasting.

Audio versions of 20 of the essays in this book, read by the
author, are collected in the CD "Blow-Drying a Chicken,"
available at www.mollyfisk.com.

Printed in the United States of America
ISBN 978-0-9894958-0-6

Dedicated to my far-flung tribe:

the family of poets.

Also by Molly Fisk

poems:

The More Difficult Beauty
Listening to Winter
Terrain (with Dan Bellm & Forrest Hamer)
Salt Water Poems (letterpress by Jungle Garden Press)

radio commentary:

Blow-Drying a Chicken (CD)
Using Your Turn Signal Promotes World Peace (CD)

Contents

WINTER

What I Want

is to inhabit
the world as it is:

the crabapple's
magenta halo

shading a squirrel
crushed into the road —

me not turning
my eyes away.

— from *The More Difficult Beauty*

SPRING

Botox

The first time I heard the word "Botox" I was sitting in my living room, teaching a poetry class, and one of my students used it in a poem. When I asked what the hell it meant, a big hue and cry was raised at my sheltered life and lack of TV-watching, and then I was informed it was a chemical injected into people's faces as a way to eliminate wrinkles.

Now let's just stop here for a minute. Despite the absence of a television, I was not born yesterday, and I know that the word "injection" is closely related to the word "needle." Putting the word "needle" and the word "face" into the same sentence is a really bad idea. Adding the word "chemical" makes it even worse. Unless there's a serious medical reason to use these words in the same sentence, I think they should be kept very far apart.

Fast forward to last week, when I went to see the new Neil Young concert movie *Heart of Gold* with my friend Max. This is a good movie if you like looking at the drooping jowls and wrinkly neck skin of 63-year-old rock singers, since that's what the camera lingers on. In time-honored tradition, Neil was the star and he had female backup singers, one of whom, I was happy to see, was Emmy Lou Harris, who can sing backup or upside-down-and-sideways and I'll listen, because her voice is amazing. At first, however, I didn't realize it was Emmy Lou — it sounded like Emmy Lou, but she didn't look like herself. She looked like Dolly Parton, without the upholstery.

Over the years, Emmy Lou has gone from an angelic and gangly hippie folksinger look to a more queenly, elegant look on stage. She's had her teeth straightened, and maybe her nose, too, I can't tell. Despite these alterations, her always-beautiful face has come into its own, and she's let her hair go gray in a wonderful progression through different stages of salt-and-pepper, which you can see if you lay her album covers out in order.

I whispered to my friend Max, "Is that Emmy Lou?" Max whispered back, "Botox." For a minute, my brain thought this was a Cajun word, maybe for a boyfriend's dress-up clothes, but then I remembered. On stage, Emmy Lou was crooning, but the only part of her face that moved was her jaw and lower lip. Everything else was completely stationary. Her eyelids closed, I noticed with relief, and then opened again. "Botox?!?" I whispered to Max. "It freezes your face so you can't move the muscles," she said.

This made me want to weep. I wish there were a way I could help the world become more just. I don't want men to get facial injections of bovine botulism, which, if it got into their bloodstreams, could kill them. I want **everyone** to revolt against the mean-spirited, sexist, economics-driven American norm that requires women to feel desperate about their looks from cradle to grave, and ties their desirability and earning power to their faces.

Neil's neck looks like a 200-year-old elephant scrotum, and he doesn't seem to mind. Why can't Emmy Lou have the same freedom?

Good Wishes

Generally, like all the women in my family,
I leap out of bed the minute I wake up, brush
my teeth while walking outside to get the paper,
hoping not too many people I know will drive by
and see me in my nightgown, and then empty the
dish-drainer while I'm waiting for the coffee water
to boil. My mother and Aunt Mary got up early so
they could have a little private time before their
families descended on them. I've come down ahead
of schedule and caught them both, in separate
kitchens, standing beside empty dish-drainers with
cups of coffee in their hands, just staring out the
window.

I don't have a family to descend on me, but
I've always felt that the early morning hours were
precious. The bird song, the way the sun slants
benignly across the world. Being up early makes
me feel as though I have money in the bank. I'm

not late yet, no one's expecting anything of me. The world is mine.

If there's a resident boyfriend around, I can be convinced to stay in bed longer, but at the moment, there isn't, and so I'm pretty spry hopping up, although I try not to disturb the cats, who tend to be sprawled all over the bedspread at daylight, after their long nights of adventure.

This morning when I woke, Bella was sleeping with her chin on my wrist. Angus had stretched his front leg across both my ankles. I lay there, happy to be useful as a prop, and looked around the bedroom.

It's a nice bedroom. Two windows, both from salvage yards, costing a total of $20. Three different colors of paint on the walls. Built-in bookcases crammed with poetry books and mysteries and old gardening magazines I think I'm going to reread. I still have my winter curtains up, the velvet ones my friend Margot made me as a house-warming gift.

The best part of my bedroom, though, is invisible. When we were near the end of remodeling the house, which was uninhabitable when I got it, I ran out of money. Some of my friends, since I was too mortified to do this, threw me a sheetrock potluck. People came with food and $7.60 for a 4x8 piece of sheetrock. The outside walls were up, and had been insulated. Most of the inside walls were still just studs and air, so you could turn sideways and slip from one room to another, which was sort of magical. My friends also brought index cards and pens, and got everyone to write good wishes for me and Scotch tape them to the insulation.

So hidden under the sheetrock and paint are 47 index cards, wishing me many poems, and true love, and good luck. I walked around with a flashlight after everyone was gone and copied these blessings down, so I wouldn't forget them. Then I did what I always do when it becomes clear that people actually love me. I cried.

Lying there this morning covered with cats, I didn't cry. I smiled. That's what I do when I think of all these people I love.

Mollyamory

Dear Diary,

Valentine's Day is coming up and once again,
I am single. Don't you think my spiritual practice
of singleness has been perfected? I'm quite sure I
could benefit from being in a relationship. I know
it would improve my patience, my compassion, and
my tolerance for other people's nutty habits. It
would help me be less arrogant and self-righteous,
things I always need to work on. I could polish my
communication skills, and practice not saving a
person who doesn't need to be saved, if you know
what I mean.

You may not be aware of the latest studies,
since you are only a diary. They show that people
in relationships have lower blood pressure because
they're touched more often. Of course, sometimes
they have really high blood pressure from being
furious at their partner, but that doesn't last very

long. People, especially the ones my age, get more exercise in relationships, and not just from having lots of sex. They walk more, as they have to move from room to room in order to hear what their loved one is saying from the couch. They get a good stretch from picking up dropped items off the floor, and increased upper-body strength from hauling two people's laundry to the washing machine.

As part of a couple, dietary habits improve dramatically. I, for one, would not want anyone to see me eating crackers and cheese for dinner while standing at the kitchen counter. Just to save face I'd buy more vegetables and actually prepare and eat them. And you know those three boxes of After Eight mints in my larder, which I stock-pile because the market doesn't always have them? They would be history.

My friend Kate says most people get in relationships because of dumb luck or low standards. I don't know about the luck part, but I try hard not to be dumb, so that makes sense. And I'm afraid I do have fairly high standards. For one thing, I'm looking for a man, and that cuts out more than half the population. I'm looking for someone who likes to talk, which cuts out another third or so. My partner will have to be old enough to know the names of all four Beatles, and young enough that he can still walk around the block unassisted. Since I'm incredibly famous within a 12-mile radius of my house, he's also going to have to not mind too much when people come up to me on the street and say, "Oh, you're the poet!"

Other than that, I'm pretty happy to take pot luck. I'm not such a snob about bad grammar as you would think, and I don't have special requirements that Mr. Wonderful know how to salsa dance or make Oysters Rockefeller.

There is one thing, though. I'm looking for a guy who wants to be with me and nobody else. The modern term for this, Dear Diary, in case you haven't heard, is Mollyamory.

Soft Porn

It is pouring with rain and a fierce wind is battering my woodpile. One of the metal lawn chairs has tumbled 20 feet and landed upside down, so it looks like an avant-garde sculpture, or it would if the lawn weren't knee-high and shaggy, half wild and half trailer park. . .

Do I care about any of this? I do not. Well, I'd vastly prefer that a tree not blow down on the house or my car. But aside from that I'm pretty oblivious. It's March. The plant and seed catalogs have just arrived and I'm lost in a daydream involving Snow Queen hydrangeas, "Blue Muffin" viburnum, and *Nepeta* "Walker's Low," otherwise known as catmint. The fantasy also involves a new planting bed with amended soil — in our landscape that means oyster shell and rock phosphate as well as good compost — and weed cloth around the edges so the darn Bermuda grass stays out, at least for a

year or two. Despite my generally practical nature,
I'm seeing in my mind's eye the newly dug-in shrubs
immediately growing to full size, white hydrangea
blossoms nodding sleepily at the ends of their arched
stems, the viburnum's deep blue berries attracting
all manner of songbirds. You get the idea.

For the moment, we won't go into the realities
of July's baking heat nor when those berries ripen,
which is probably **not** while the hydrangeas are
flowering. In gardening daydreams, everything is
possible and someone else has always figured out the
soil's Ph and dug the planting holes.

These catalogs are designed to sell us a fantasy,
and they do their work well. This photo here, of
Passiflora "Sherry" for instance, spilling out of its
frame, really might as well be a 23-year-old with
his shirt off, smiling at us over a bronzed shoulder.
And the copy! Listen to this: "'Sherry' is the first
of the new Darkhorse series of Passionflower
hybrids. Its blooms are an intense ruby red with
black-and-white-speckled filaments, a breathtaking
sight climbing a trellis." The mind turns
smoothly to other things in life that blush red
and how nimbly a 23-year-old could climb a trellis
conveniently located, say, under your bedroom
window. Breathtaking, indeed. . . Dear Reader,

I will leave the speckled filaments to your agile
imagination.

Page after page of this kind of seduction
and it's no wonder we haul out our wallets to
purchase Phlox "Purple Kiss" and "Gypsy Love,"
Hemerocallis "Black Stockings" (which looks like
a daylily to me), Coreopsis "Autumn Blush," and
Delphinium "Wishful Thinking!" All by itself, spring
makes you want to tear off your clothes and join the
great fertility dance. Add soft gardening porn to the
mix and who knows what will happen?

This morning's rain, however, has just turned to
heavy snow. I'd better get my boots on, find a broom,
and go thump the branches of my fruit trees so
they don't break off. The brave daffodils are bowing
white heads now, and the woodpile suddenly looks
too small to last the rest of the winter.

Sigh. Early March. No 23-year-olds in sight.

The Berliners' Copper Beech

I'm looking out the window at the most beautiful tree in Nevada County. It's a copper beech in new leaf, dripping with rain. Probably a hundred years old, with a trunk that's six feet around. Its lowest branches drape almost to the ground, like dark skirts. I think it may be the only copper beech in the county, at least it's the only one I've ever been able to find, and I've looked hard — this is mostly an eastern genus. I first met its sisters in Cambridge's Mount Auburn Cemetery. Those specimens are probably twice as old. I like to think some pioneer carried a beechnut to California and planted it next to her tent on a mining claim.

This tree shades the white clapboard house of Harold and Mary Ann Berliner, a couple who've lived in this county for more than half the tree's life. After a while they stopped building benches around its trunk because the seats kept busting when the trunk grew. According to Mary Ann, their eight children played in its branches, and swept up the nuts every fall. No young trees have ever sprouted under the canopy.

We're talking about the tree this morning because we both love it, and because we've already talked about Harold's death. He passed away on Sunday, at the age of 86, but I heard about it only this morning. I drove over to see if a visit might be welcome or anything needed to be done. I'm nominally a friend of Mary Ann's daughter Judith — I've spent very little one-on-one time with Mary Ann, but she's a woman you connect with or you don't, for life, and I did.

Harold was a lawyer and the District Attorney for Nevada county for 17 years, as well as a world-renowned printer and type designer. In 1968, when the Supreme Court established the Miranda rights, he was asked to help write a simple warning that D.A.s could read to suspects, resulting in the famous wording we all know from TV and films: "You have the right to remain silent. Anything you say can and will be used against you. . ." He printed and sold hundreds of thousands of wallet-sized cards so the words would be at hand when people needed them.

My relationship with Harold was similar to the one I had with my great-aunts: 80% of it revolved around grammar — mostly his delight in correcting mine. Split infinitives, dangling participles, spelling errors, lack of agreement: nothing was beyond his eagle eye, and because I'm a writer he got extra glee from finding mistakes in pieces already aired or published and wrote to me immediately to point them out. We turned this into kind of a shtick — I never knowingly goofed up or failed to correct some blooper I found myself, but when I realized I'd made a mistake, I kept track of how long it took him to discover it. I was not Harold's only student. On one of the last days of his life, when everyone thought he was asleep, he opened his eyes suddenly and reminded a granddaughter to be vigilant about her grammar.

In small towns like ours, personalities and place get all tangled together. Someone like Harold Berliner makes a big difference, both in life and in death. While Mary Ann and the kids and grandkids mourn a personal loss, the rest of us suffer a civic one. Just like we'll never know who planted the copper beech beside the house, with Harold's passing a part of our mutual history is now out of reach, unrecoverable.

Keeping Secrets

Keeping secrets gives me a stomach-ache. In my youth I liked the way a secret made me feel: as though I were James Bond, or Illya Kuryakin. Knowing something other people didn't was a sign of importance and power. But somewhere along the way secrets started to seem mean-spirited. Now, when people ask, "Can you keep a secret?" I say, "**No**. I can't. Whatever it is, **don't** tell me!" This startles them, but it works.

I don't want to know if you're having an affair, or someone else is having an affair, or somebody has cancer or AIDS. That so-and-so is living on a trust fund or whosits is on the verge of bankruptcy is just none of my business. In the first place, knowing secrets like this means that I see the interested parties differently, and that's annoying. I turn self-conscious around them, can't be fully myself, and keep thinking about the secret instead of reality. It interferes with my ability to be open.

In the second place, knowing secrets ties up brain cells that would be more profitably engaged in writing poems, or planning a birthday party for my niece. I need all the brain-cells I can muster these days — using some up for reasons that don't have anything to do with my life is just silly. Plus, remembering not to tell the secret takes a lot of energy.

In the third place, in my experience whenever there's a secret, someone eventually gets hurt. Probably not the secret's instigator, and probably not the confidante. Some third party — the husband who's being cheated on or the child of the person with cancer — is going to find out the secret eventually and feel duped and betrayed by not having known all along. Just writing this reminds me of the summer of 1974, when I discovered a man I was in love with was having a romance with my sister. My whole family knew, but none of them told me. That took a long time to get over, and as you see, 39 years later, I haven't forgotten.

Secrets ruin relationships and tear families apart. They bust up friendships and mar the workplace. They rend holes in the social fabric of the community. I think we should revolt against them.

If you're carrying any secrets at the moment, get rid of them: just blurt them out to the next person you meet. I want grocery aisles and church pews and minor league baseball bleachers to fill with the sound of spilled secrets. Tell them all, and then take a deep breath. No guilt allowed. You're not betraying the person who told you, you're helping us all return to our own concerns and the present moment, which is where we belong.

There are other ways to feel like Illya Kuryakin. Put on a black turtleneck and practice your Russian accent.

Dancing School

For some unknown reason I woke up this morning thinking about Dancing School. The place hasn't crossed my mind in 40 years — I have no idea what dream or scent or combination of invisible factors brought the memory back today. I imagine memory as a juke box, and sometimes when you push the buttons it's not the right 45 that drops into place, but the one next to it. In my head, anyway, the records are filed in random order. So I was probably preparing to recall oatmeal, anticipating breakfast, but got Dancing School instead.

I'm not talking about a ballet school for little girls, or the modern dance classes I took on Union Street. Dancing School, capital D, capital S, was where kids of my age (13) and class (upper middle) and race (white) and religion (not the predominantly Jewish kids of my school, but the scattering of Protestants) learned to foxtrot and waltz in San Francisco.

Classes were held at the swanky California
Club downtown. Girls had to wear dresses and
white gloves, boys suits and ties. If I was 13 this
was 1968, a strange time in history to be practicing
the waltz, since the rest of the city was listening
to Grace Slick in Golden Gate Park and learning
to inhale. Nevertheless, I waited outside our house
on Divisadero on Tuesday nights after supper for
the carpool, fervently hoping the snaps on my
garter belt didn't spontaneously unhook themselves
from my stockings and cause the kind of acute
embarrassment I spent most of puberty dreading.
Pantyhose had not yet been invented. This is
something you don't hear much about: the terror of
girls for the strange layers of undergarments they
have to learn to manage. God forbid you got your
period on a Dancing School day and had to wrangle
both garter belt and menstrual pad belt and then
not trip over your partner's feet doing the Cha-cha-
cha. We were too young for tampons, which were
rumored among eighth graders to make you not a
virgin any more, and were therefore shunned.

The biggest revelation of Dancing School
wasn't *The Blue Danube*, it was that boys could
sweat through their hands. Our gloves left palms
and fingers dry in a kind of clammy way when we

stripped them off in somebody's mother's car on
the way home. The boys had no protection and
regularly left wet hand prints on our dresses at
waist level. If you liked the boy this could be taken
in stride, but usually we didn't like the ones who
sweated overtly — 8th grade is all about keeping
your cool — and groaned in disgust when they
chose us as partners. Girls are like baby sharks —
they'll tear apart whoever's already bleeding.

I'm no longer 13 or upper middle class, and aside
from the odd wedding, don't do much waltzing.
But recently someone pulled me into his arms
and twirled me around a dance floor, refreshing
my memory of those three steps into corners of
an imaginary box on the ground, the proprietary
embrace, the spinning and turning. I've gotten
better at following over the years, and much less
self-conscious. Neither of our hands began to sweat.
And it's interesting what kind of music you can end
up waltzing to.

Even — if you're not too stoned — the Jefferson
Airplane.

The Hero

One of the reasons I never committed suicide when I was recovering my incest memories is that I was so fascinated to think a part of my own brain could be hidden from me and then suddenly appear.

Before my own memories returned, I'd never heard of memory repression. I didn't know anyone who'd been molested, either. When these weird scenes first began to come into my head — not full-blown scenes, really, but images — accompanied by creepy feelings, I had no idea what was going on. Why, on a sunny winter morning while I was doing the dishes, would an image of wide-wale corduroy fill my entire field of vision? What was so terrifying about corduroy near my face that it would cause me to burst into tears and lose my grip on a plate, letting it fall into the sink and shatter?

The only flashbacks I'd ever heard of were acid flashbacks, so I thought maybe I was having one,

since I did take LSD in the '70s. But none of those
acid trips had any terror in them, or any corduroy,
either. Mostly on acid I thought my neck was
growing, like a giraffe.

Besides the fear and puzzling images, suddenly
for no reason I'd go into fight-or-flight mode. It's one
thing to do this when a car's coming too fast toward
the crosswalk you're in, but when it happens while
you're washing your hair, it's very confusing. At that
time I didn't know any Viet Nam vets and had never
heard of Post traumatic stress. I just thought I was
losing my mind.

I've been smart since I was a little girl. Figuring
things out and getting good grades meant a lot to
me, and my brain, rather than my looks or athletic
prowess, was what I got by on. To think that it
might be failing me was horrible. Luckily, one day
a woman I know discovered me crying and shaking,
rooted to the linoleum in the Pepperidge Farm aisle
of our local grocer's. She was a District Attorney,
and had prosecuted cases involving repressed
memory, so she knew some of the signs.

Once I had an idea to explore, a possible name
for what seemed to be wrong, my faithful brain got
to work, analyzing everything. I'd have to say the
next five years were worse than you can imagine,

but every time I got ready to slit my wrists or drive my car off the road, my brain would say, "Wait! There's more — don't you want to know how the story ends?"

It took a total of 20 years to get to the last page. It's not a happy ending, exactly, but at least nobody died. I still have Post traumatic stress, but much less often, and I get over it faster. I've learned a ton about human nature: the good, the bad, the evil. I wouldn't wish incest, or recovering from it, on anyone.

But I'm really glad I'm the sort of person who wants to know how the story ends — especially since I turn out to be the hero.

Coffee-Shop Morality

It's 8 a.m. and I'm sitting in my favorite café. My friends behind the counter are making scones, decorating Easter cookies, and foaming milk for various coffee drinks ordered by the people in front of the counter. Right now the line is four customers long, but the high school kids are walking toward us across the parking lot, so it will swell to 15 in a minute.

When you live alone, which I do, and you're a gregarious person, you have to go out into the world to get your social fix. These days I get a lot of social interaction from Facebook, but dealing with a screen is essentially unsatisfactory for humans, because it uses only one of our senses, sight. Although we imagine ourselves as thinking beings, and we do cogitate a lot, 21st century humans still operate like our ancestors did: by sense. Sight, sound, taste, texture, and smell rule our brains. They give us the information that we later think **about.** If you curtail sensory input, no matter how much of a genius you are, at some point your thinking becomes shallow and circular for lack of replenishing. That's my theory, anyway. If you look around any office building you'll see it in action. A palpable malaise hangs over those cubicles like smog.

Remember in third grade, when all the kids put on their raincoats and found a buddy to hold hands with walking down the street toward the natural history museum? Teachers know that field trips are a great way to inspire and also distract their students from getting too cooped up in the classroom. Leaving those four walls and smelling some subway brake fumes, or the damp air underneath redwoods, changes a person's mood entirely. Looking at pigeons, at other people in line at the museum, hearing all the unfamiliar noises and feeling a breeze on your arm and sun or rain on your head instead of fluorescent lighting is incredibly reviving.

My venturing out to a favorite coffee shop is like a field trip in my working day — even though it's familiar, every time I go there are different people to talk to, a cacophony of smells and sounds that I don't have at home, and I usually get into some sort of discussion about a subject I would never have imagined.

Today the subject is ethics. Apparently a customer has been ordering three shots of espresso, which costs $2.80, in a large cup, and then filling her cup with cream from the counter where the cream and sugar and lids are. If she had ordered a three-shot "breve" from the staff, which is the exact same ingredients: espresso and cream, it would cost $5.25, a price based on the prices of those ingredients. The cream on the counter is there to use in your coffee, and most people take a small amount, so there's no reason to charge them. But this customer is using close to a cup, and shorting the cafe $2.45.

This is a great subject. You can see the owner's point of view: ingredients need to be paid for or she'll go out of business. You can kind of see the customer's angle: coffee drinks are expensive and the cream on the counter is free so why not lower the price of the drink by using it? And you can employ your senses: watching the barista's frown as she rings up the sale, cash register tinkling. The glug glug as the cream is poured into a kind of watchful hush, the scents of just-ground coffee and fresh scones mingling overhead.

When you go out into the world, you run smack up against the moral issues of life, played out right in front of you. I'm going to take this dilemma back to Facebook and see what my friends think...

ABCDEFG

    I asked a librarian friend of mine the other day if she sings the alphabet song when she's cataloguing books. I always sing it as I peruse library shelves for new mysteries, or look things up in the dictionary.

    Whenever I mention this song to people, I am met not with raised eyebrows and haughty looks, but with other songs and mnemonics. This same librarian recited phrases whose first letters spelled out Arithmetic and Geography. Someone I went to school with reminded me that My Very Elegant Mother Just Sat Upon Nine Pizzas was the way we'd been taught the order of the planets as they circle the sun. I can still sing you, but I won't, a little math song I learned in fifth grade to remind us what the square of the hypotenuse of a right triangle is equal to.

    I can't tell you how happy it makes me to know that our childhoods are still inside us like this. I

don't recall much else from grade school, which
makes me wonder about the power of both music
and memorizing. For me, sound and repetition are
the big transporters. Proust had his madeleines,
but I have Neil Young wailing "Southern Man" and
immediately I'm back at the kitchen table, trying to
write a report on Nicaragua as the rest of the family
mills around and California's winter rain sluices
down the glass doors.

Our music teacher single-handedly dragged the
whole eighth grade through a year of rehearsals to
perform Gilbert and Sullivan's *H.M.S. Pinafore*,
which — 44 years later — I could probably sing you
at least two-thirds of, if you paid me a lot and had a
couple hours to spare.

I tell my writing students not to memorize
anything they don't really love, because what they
learn by heart will get into their bloodstreams and
start coming out of their own pens and pencils. Even
if you're not a writer, I think what you commit to
memory matters. My niece, Gioia, recently leaned
forward in the car and recited "Jabberwock" into
my ear; she knew it perfectly. When I bragged
about her to my ex-boyfriend, he reeled off the
first lines himself without missing a beat. It made
me so jealous! But she's a Waldorf student, not

the norm. I worry what will become of us when
knowing dialogue from *Star Wars* movies by heart
replaces the Gettysburg Address in our national
consciousness. Maybe it already has.

You are probably still wondering about the
librarian. "Of course I sing the alphabet song,"
she said, "especially between G and M." I was
delighted to hear this. There's a lot of conflict in our
country right now — red states versus blue ones,
the fundamentalist right-wing Christians against
the emphatic and outraged Liberals. It gives me a
little hope to think that library patrons and staff all
across America are wandering through the aisles,
united in muttering under their breath: "A B C D E
F G, H I J K LMNO P..."

Losing Utah

This morning I stood under some cedar trees with a cat named Ned in my arms and watched a friend's body lifted from his bed onto the mortuary's gurney. The rest of his family waited on the other side of the house, to take charge of the gurney. The old family dog was positioned so he would trip people on the path, although everyone managed to maneuver around him.

I don't have a good explanation for why I stayed in view of the bedroom door — I had a strong feeling that someone needed to watch this transfer of body from bed to gurney. Perhaps it was base curiosity — death being so strange. I wanted to keep an eye on my friend for as long as he was with us, to give him a continuous witness. I'm never going to see him again. Some part of me wanted to look as long as I was allowed, even as he was wrapped in his own bedsheets, seat-belted in, and covered with a blanket. I never saw his face.

In a way, it was ridiculous. The body did not contain my friend any more, that was very clear. It was a husk, a carapace that had been discarded. But still, I stood there, stroking the cat and watching the gurney's wheels as they caught on a flower pot and then were disentangled, noting the dusting of star-lily pollen that clung to the seat of one attendant's brown pants where she'd brushed up against a flower arrangement. My friend was delivered into the hands of his children, the perfect place for him to be. They carried him down the path, past the house's glass front doors and the patio table where we'd eaten so many summer dinners. Past blue hydrangeas, and many, many forget-me-nots, through the little slatted gate and into the back of a white van.

On the record player, Luciano Pavarotti was singing Puccini at the top of his lungs. It was a song my friend loved. He also loved the thought of playing very loud music as a person is carried out of the house for the last time. It was part of a story he told about one of his own mentors, and seemed perfectly natural to repeat when his time came.

We watched the van until it turned out of sight, and then milled around in the garden, crying and not crying in different configurations. The old dog, seeing the gate open, tried to sneak off down the street where there are some chickens he would like to devour. He was not successful.

My friend was unusually charismatic: opinionated, funny, convincing. Someone with memorable integrity. There is such a huge difference between his alive self and his dead one that my brain can't make the leap. Maybe that's why so many traditions suggest the bereaved wear black for a year and stay away from ordinary social events. It takes that long to get used to the notion that someone is truly gone.

Good-bye, sweet rowdy friend. Thank you for everything.

Cat Lady?

Everyone thinks I'm one of those cat ladies. "Crazy" cat ladies, I believe they're called. People with many dogs are called breeders, or Lord and Lady Grantham if they live at Downton Abbey. People with sheep, goats, and cows are farmers. No one calls the aquarium-lover a "crazy fish lady," no matter how many Siamese fighting bettas she has. And the adjective seems to attach itself to "lady" rather than "gentleman." Let's be charitable and assume that's because of the rhyme.

I do love cats. They're smart, soft, incredibly funny, and wash themselves — what's not to love? As a human with a tendency to get lonely, I don't want one cat, all by itself when I leave the house. I want my cats to be happy, and for that they need their own kind. Right now I have five, due to my tendency to adopt whole families. I lost two this winter to predators, which happens despite my

Jurassic Park-like fencing arrangement over half the yard. Sometimes they manage to escape via pear tree and blackberry bush.

I cherish and protect my own cats. I'm also fond of other people's: friends' cats, bookstore cats, the little black one I spoke to for ten minutes Saturday night on someone's lawn in Berkeley. I am not, however, a "slut" for cats. I'm currently locked in ferocious combat with one particular feline, and I'm losing.

He's a stray, and "intact," as they say, who looks and acts like Norman Mailer: burly and swaggering, with a big square head. After we put the miraculous six-foot wire fence up — the fence no one could get in or out of — he started showing up to gorge on Science Diet and pick fights with my males. It took weeks to figure out he just climbed a fence pole and threw himself onto the lawn with abandon. He lolls around on my deck in the sun. I come home and he's on the sofa. After seven failed attempts, I've given up trying to catch him in the county's Have-a-Heart trap. If he were nice, I'd just adopt him. But he's not nice. He expresses himself very clearly by spraying anything I've touched. This morning, his stench gilded the microwave, the bread box, a geranium pot, and clean laundry in the basket I had foolishly left in the kitchen. It's pouring with rain, but my doors are wide open. I've wiped things down with hydrogen peroxide where possible. Last month, when it was warm, my car windows were open all night — he hit steering wheel, dash, and back seat upholstery. He sprays the wood pile. I am losing my mind.

It's hard to know how to deal with a true foe. I pray some bobcat will eat him, but until then I'm trying to adopt the strategy of the Dalai Lama. His Holiness calls the Chinese, who for decades have trashed Tibet, "my friend, the enemy."

SUMMER

Does Birdsong Really Enlarge Your Garden?

Sometimes I wake in the morning and it's still dark. I can't tell which cat is curled against my ribs, nor see the outline of the windows yet, and except for the engine of a truck whose headlights angle through the room as it speeds past my mailbox, there's total silence. The calm, as they say, before the storm.

If I don't fall back to sleep, I like to lie there and wait for my favorite band to start playing. Sweeter than the Grateful Dead, more raucous than the Gipsy Kings, and even older than the Rolling Stones, the dawn chorus of song birds begins before I can see any light at all, and lasts until every blossom on every branch is clearly visible. It's a wonderful melee, a beautiful cacophony, both melodic and chaotic, a crazy din. It reminds me of the way Utah Phillips sometimes ended his concerts. He'd announce it was time to sing the People's National Anthem, and before his audience could get ready to protest, he'd have everyone standing up singing their own favorite song at the top of their lungs, in unison. The noise went beyond horrible into some unexpected joyous place, and that's where the bird chorus goes, too.

The average bird has a wide range and repertoire. No one quite knows why dawn is the designated hour for birdsong bliss, although they think singing has to do with claiming territory and attracting mates. Sound carries almost 20 times farther at dawn than at midday, so it's an effective broadcasting hour, and because it isn't light yet, birds can't start foraging, so there isn't that distraction.

Yesterday I heard a marvelous thing I'm still trying to find out more about. Supposedly, when birdsong begins at dawn, the small cells on the undersides of plant leaves, called stomata, open in response to the sound. Plants absorb nutrients through their leaves this way, so the more open the stomata, the more food they'll take in, and the larger they'll grow. If you cut down bird habitat around a garden or farm, thereby reducing the bird population, your plants won't grow as large, lush, and productively as they otherwise would.

Some curious human being, of course, worked out a replication of birdsong to see what happens if you play MORE sounds and convince the stomata to stay open longer. Using a cassette that included Vivaldi's Spring movement from *The Four Seasons*, Indian ragas, and Bach's *Violin Concerto in E-major*, this guy claims to increase growth by 500 - 700% this way. Ottawa University researchers broadcast Bach's violin concertos to a wheat field during one experiment, and reportedly increased the size of the wheat grains by 66%.

While I love the idea that birdsong influences plant health and productivity, the jury's still out here at my house. The grass is a little taller, and my peonies are huge this year, but the lavender looks sort of puny.

The cats, I'm happy to report, are the same size they've always been.

Hammer & Nails

I just went to visit a friend and discovered
that the roof was off half her house and large men
were clambering around on scaffolding, putting
up a new one. There were thick laminated beams
and gargantuan headers, and it was hot. The guys
had their shirts off and were basting in the sun,
under a crust of sweat and sawdust. My friend and
I and the dogs sat in the shade and watched the
proceedings.

As someone who earns a living with her head,
I've always been amazed to see houses being built.
People like you and me actually make them out of
vacant lots. One day there's a lot of bindweed and
crabgrass, maybe some broken bottles. Then, six
months later — after many trips to the lumber yard,
and a certain amount of swearing — there's a house,
with doors that lock, windows with screens, and
indoor plumbing. It's incredible!

We sat there, admiring the agility of these guys and the fullness of their moustaches. We decided we really **couldn't** interrupt their work to offer sunscreen — we would never be taken seriously again. One disappeared around the corner and came back a few minutes later with two rafters. He leaned them against the existing wall, climbed the scaffolding, pulled one up after him, traded two short sentences with his pal, and bam! A rafter nailed in place, its notches fitted over the beams just so, the nails pounded by hand and not with a nail gun. No muss, no fuss.

I almost married a man who had sustained a bad head injury, so watching people dance around on small boards 8 feet in the air makes my stomach roll over, but these two seemed to have things well in hand, and besides, as they pointed out, under the sawdust and dropped nails the room whose roof they had torn off was still carpeted, so they had a little padding if they needed it.

When we were working on my house, which had to be gutted and put together again before I could live in it, I attempted to nail a few things. Rodger, the guy in charge, kept insinuating that I sounded like a very old, possibly dying woodpecker, and eventually I took the hint and shifted to tasks where my expertise was more appreciated: writing checks, jack-hammering concrete, choosing sinks. I can prime and paint with the best of 'em, spackle, hose things down, drive to the dump. I'm a whiz at choosing unmatched windows from the salvage yard. But I could probably **knit** a house faster than I could build one out of wood.

Not being handy with a hammer is one of my regrets, like not being any good at turning cartwheels. But I haven't given up yet. One of these days, all by myself, I'm going to build something out of wood and nails that's big enough to stand up in.

You'll know I've begun when you hear the tapping of a **very** healthy woodpecker.

In Sickness and in Health

Once upon a time, in a galaxy far, far away, I
was a bridesmaid 11 times in one year. Not all of
those weddings required me to buy the famous
never-to-be-worn-again dress, but many of them
did. I attended dress fittings, bridal showers,
rehearsals, and rehearsal dinners — where the job
of bridesmaid was to make sure the groom's great-
aunt Myrtle had someone to talk to — and then the
wedding itself.

I was sometimes promoted from bridesmaid
to maid-of-honor. I love these archaic terms. Maid
doesn't mean servant in this case, it means virgin.
And honor I suppose has to do with being most
honored among the maids, though I always secretly
thought, especially in the 70s, it meant you had to
be honorable and not seduce the groom.

When I was six I was a flower girl at my Aunt
Amanda's wedding, and besides these 11 times in

one year, I've served as a bridesmaid eight or ten more, so I have been in my share of weddings, thank you, taking all the female parts except for bride and mother-of-the-bride or -groom.

I've mentioned before that I have a slight inferiority complex about never having been married — it makes me feel like a social outcast. I don't dwell on this, particularly, but when I go to some one else's wedding it does cross my mind. So it was very interesting to find myself last weekend at the end of the aisle, not preceding the bride, but watching her walk toward me. When the bride asked me to officiate, I was startled, but said yes. It was an honor to be asked. I got my Universal Life Church license and looked up ceremonies on the Internet. The happy couple and I met twice, wrote out what they wanted, and then I rehearsed. It was sort of like getting ready for a poetry reading, which I can do in my sleep.

But I was completely unprepared for what it felt like to be responsible for marrying this couple. Even when I got to the wedding site — a calm grove of trees near Lake Tahoe — I still didn't understand. It wasn't until they walked down the aisle and stood before me, facing each other, that my stomach rolled over. They couldn't get married without me! Unless

I read the ceremony and prompted them in their vows it wasn't going to happen. *How can this be? I thought. I've never been married! I know nothing about for richer or for poorer and in sickness or in health!* I almost burst into tears at how much trust they had in me. But I didn't. Luckily, I pulled myself together. Everyone else can weep at a wedding, but the officiant is supposed to be cool. I was incredibly cool. Catholic priests aren't married, after all, and they've been doing this for centuries.

I took a deep breath and said everything in the right order, and made sure they both answered "I do." Then, by the power vested in me, I pronounced them husband and wife. They kissed, and walked down the aisle away from me to wild applause.

It was great! It was just like a real wedding.

Potlucks

Although I'm usually a mild-mannered, well-behaved, poet-of-a-certain-age, happy to let you go first when we come to a stop sign at the same moment, occasionally I snap. Snap as in break in half, like a twig. Snap as in go for your jugular vein with my big white saber-tooth teeth. Metaphorically speaking, of course, but the energy is similar. Suddenly, something happens and it's just too much, the last straw has descended on the camel's back and the camel throws off her burden of silk rugs and starts to trample the tents.

The oddest things will provoke me, but they often involve some sort of inequity. Take, for instance, potlucks. What could possibly irk a girl about a potluck, you ask? Well, how about the famous potluck-gender-inequity pandemic? You know what I mean. The home-made lasagne and Waldorf salad versus store-bought salsa and a bag

of chips? Or maybe just the bag of chips? Now I
know I'm making a generalization here: all women
do not cook and all men do not pick things up at
7-11 on their way to the party. Richard brought a
great carrot cake to the last meal I attended, and
Rodger often loads Moroccan delicacies into his
Tupperware. But it's not a **gross** generalization.
And I'm thoroughly sick of it. Since I can't change
anyone else's behavior, I'm changing my own. No
more Molly's Grandmother's Famous Chocolate
Cake this summer, unless you'd like to borrow the
recipe. I'm going to man up for potlucks. I'll bring
the tonic, the limes, the Smart Food, or maybe a box
of Altoids.

I started my new campaign last weekend by
buying an angel food cake at Safeway. My mistake
was doing this in advance. After looking at it on my
counter for a few hours in its see-through plastic
container, I broke down. The cake looked so lonely. . .
So I slapped it onto a pretty blue plate, whipped up a
glaze out of butter, lemon juice, and powdered sugar,
went outside, clipped a few flowers and put a drinking
glass in the cake's central hole for a vase. It took 45
minutes, and the cake and I both felt so much better!

But of course, it wasn't guy-like behavior. And
here's why. I wanted people to **like** me. I didn't

want them to sneer at my offering or think it was lame, I wanted **praise** for my efforts. This is a big deterrent to being a potluck man. Next time I will praise myself for not wasting time on idiotic things like flowers, and buy the cake on the way to the party, so there's no time to anthropomorphize its feelings.

"Potluck" is mostly a western idea, according to Wikipedia — as in west of the Rockies, not the opposite of Asia. It's thought to be related to "potlatch," the elaborate shared feast of Northwestern Indian tribes that involved a spirit of generosity and maybe a little competition. The name also has roots in the Southern American phrase of "taking potluck," or joining someone for whatever's already cooking. I've always liked the randomness of potlucks — how you really don't know if a balanced meal awaits you. It could be 17 loaves of French bread and a pitcher of Bloody Marys.

I hope my diatribe inspires you to shake things up. If you always work hard on a dish and are feeling a little put-upon, pick up a bottle of wine this time, or a watermelon. Do **not** carve the melon into the shape of a swan and fill it with rum-infused fruit salad! Just bring the darn

melon. Your host will surely have a knife. And
if you're a last-minute, what-if-it's-a-potluck?
individual, maybe this is the day to challenge
yourself with Beef Wellington.

Me, I'm on my way over right now. Can't wait to
see you! Just got to stop at the gas station for those
Altoids. . .

Gutter Girl

When I told a friend where I was last night, she said if she'd been offered a million dollars she never would have guessed. So I've successfully fooled at least one person into thinking I'm not into bowling. And most of the time, I'm not. But every now and then someone suggests it, for a birthday party or a lark, and I'm surprised all over again by how much fun it is.

When I was a banker in Chicago, lots of us went bowling after work. Some of those people were real sharks! They'd take off the suit jackets, roll up their sleeves, and bowl strike after strike. In that crowd I was comic relief — someone who could so consistently **miss** hitting any pins at all, they named me Gutter Girl. It was a blast, and I did get better with practice, although I never lost the nickname. That was 30 years ago, and the intervening time off has not improved my game. I've also stopped drinking and come to find out that sobriety is a big impediment to really good bowling.

There's one bowling alley in our town, with the encouraging name of "Prosperity Lanes." The time to go is five o'clock. You plunk down your money for an hour and rent those funny two-tone shoes. It's one of the only times I wear communal shoes and I always say a little prayer that my socks will protect me from cooties. I hope I'm not unduly fastidious, but I really don't want any cooties. Then I buy a glass of ice water because it's nice to have something to wet your whistle, and choose a bowling ball. I try hard not to let the different colors influence me, and luckily the ten-pound balls, which seem the right weight for me, are a lovely metallic burgundy. One hates to be too girly about these things but I bowl less well if my ball is an ugly color. In the interest of full-girliness disclosure, I confess that I choose socks to wear bowling that will match the rented shoes, too.

I have no idea how the scoring works, so whoever I'm with has to be in charge of that, but I do pick a good pseudonym. It's very bad luck to bowl under your own name. I'm usually Ruby or Pearl, sometimes Ethel — a nice '50s moniker.

Once these preliminaries are out of the way, it's time to hurl that ball down the lane. I've been told it's good to keep your thumb up, so I do, although this doesn't distract my balls from their magnetic attraction to the gutter — either gutter: I seem to be ambi-gutter-ous. I can't tell you what last night's score was because we muffed keeping track at some point. But I got two spares, and both of them were really strikes — where I knocked all the pins down in one go — that just had bad timing. I did a little victory dance in the aisle.

Despite not being an expert, I love bowling. When else do we get to play any more? So if someone offers you a million dollars to guess what I'm doing on a Wednesday night, now you know. After you've picked up the money, come join us: Bowling is good for the soul.

Bruce Willis

Alright, it's now officially too hot. I know it's
not as hot as it was last summer, and I'm grateful,
but it's still too hot to walk on asphalt, too hot to
grip the steering wheel, too hot to stop and talk to
friends on the street. When it gets this hot I spend
a lot of time at the library. I nurse iced tea for hours
at local cafés, dawdle in the frozen foods aisle at the
market. I admit it — I'm a slut for air conditioning.

Last week it got so hot I resorted to a matinée.
I went to see Bruce Willis in *Live Free or Die
Hard*. This movie — the first to use a state motto
in its title, thank you New Hampshire — was
fascinating. I had no idea it was so hard to blow up
a studio apartment.

Women are advised not to attend Bruce
Willis movies on their own, so I went with my
friend Dawn. Neither of us is in love with Bruce,
but we both belong to a small and fast-growing

demographic of the middle-aged female movie-
going public — we love explosions. I think there's
a sociological reason for this, although I haven't
checked it out with Dawn. By age 45, most American
women have done too many dishes and made too
many beds. We've had it. But because we were well-
brought-up, we don't just torch our houses and light
out for the territories. Instead, we sublimate and go
to explosion movies.

And really, where else are you going to learn
how to bring a helicopter down out of the sky using
only your car?! It's actually easier than it sounds:
Bruce gave a great demonstration. First you let your
passenger out in the nearest available tunnel, so the
helicopterists don't shoot him. Then, while driving
slowly, you open your door slightly and aim the
car at a Jersey barrier or some other large object.
A detached garage would work just fine. As the
helicopter dips down to see what you're up to, you
floor the engine and leap out, rolling in front of the
large object and saving yourself, while your car hits
the thing, flips up on its nose, and, using only its
taillights, cleverly creams the helicopter! This makes
a truly beautiful fireball.

If you want to practice this at home, I recommend
doing the somersaults and swearing part before you

bring the car into it. Then just rehearse diving out of the car door without a large object nearby — let the car roll to a stop on your neighbor's lawn. Once you've got that down, you're ready — all you need is some megalomaniac to send a helicopter after you, and that isn't hard to arrange.

Bruce Willis is a little too cocky for me, but I like a guy who hangs out with his ex-wife and her new 17-years-younger husband. You know his kids matter more to him than anyone's opinion of his virility. I also like the fact that behind his smirk he looks so exhausted. Well, if you'd spent all afternoon dangling by one hand from an SUV that somehow became suspended in an elevator shaft, you'd be worn out, too, I suppose.

Even if it wasn't 98 degrees in the shade.

Happy Birthday to Me!

I just had a very mellow and satisfying birthday. Nothing major happened — I saw people I love, talked to others on the phone, went swimming, took in several hours of a music festival, and was treated to dinner. The only surprise, really, was that I got a little goofy on Facebook. Three weeks beforehand I started announcing how many shopping days there were until my birthday — which is originally a line from the Peanuts cartoons. Facebook is a funny place. Some of the things we post are totally ignored, while others seem to hit a sweet spot and provoke lots of response. Me talking about my birthday turned out to be hugely entertaining for some reason.

I've almost always liked my own birthdays and not gotten snarled in a web of expectations or a detailed review of regrets. Also, I come from a family that likes a good running joke. So I cheerfully

reminded everyone that my birthday was almost
here, and presents began to arrive at my door.
Somewhere along the line I had mentioned colorful
watering cans from a local store, hoping to promote
them because the store is one of my Facebook
clients. And I made a wisecrack about hating black
licorice. I received TWO watering cans, one orange,
one pink, which was perfect — two I can use. More
would have been too many. The night of my birthday
someone left red licorice at my door.

This whole thing could have gotten out of hand,
but luckily it didn't. I wasn't trying to rake in
birthday loot, I was trying to cheer everyone up and
be funny. I ended up receiving a modest number of
excellent presents, all from people I know pretty well,
and getting hundreds of good wishes on Facebook.
Looking back and being perfectly honest with myself,
I think what I really wanted for my birthday was
attention, and I got that in glorious abundance.

Now that it's five shopping days PAST my
birthday, or 360 until the next one, I'm back in my
ordinary life: cat barf on the rug, clean laundry
wrinkling in the basket, and nothing in the icebox
but peanut butter and wilted spinach. Speaking
of birthdays, though, two women I know are due
to have babies in the middle of August. They've

gotten to that last Jiffy Pop stage where it seems impossible their bellies could expand any more, but suddenly they do. Their faces hold the luminous beauty pregnancy brings, even when they're rolling their eyes in exasperation that there's still a whole month to go.

And on the other end of life, one of my friends is in his last days with us. His skin has taken on an alabaster translucence and there's a distance in his eyes that comes and goes, as if he can see things the rest of us don't know are there. He's beginning to forget words and sometimes just abandons a thought and moves on. All the things he's been intending to do are falling away. When I visit him — to read poems or kibitz — I think how we're all going to be doing this, sooner or later, slowly or fast: letting go our hold on this world, its to-do lists and birthday candles, its willows reflecting evening light into the pond.

I feel incredibly sad to watch him go, and at the same time I wonder what it's like. When my time comes, I hope I can do it with as much equanimity as a birthday.

Blow-Drying a Chicken

Yesterday at the dentist, getting my teeth cleaned again because my flossing schedule seems to be alternate Thursdays under a blue moon, I had a wonderful exchange with the hygienist. It started with small talk about spring, how great it's not raining, now we can plant our gardens, that sort of thing. In the odd moments of rest between baring my teeth like a chimpanzee to receive all her jabbings and stabbings, I confessed that I grow tomatoes, really — maybe some squash or pumpkins, but nothing else thrives. She said corn was a ridiculous waste of time for the two or three ears you get, when it's a dollar for five organic ears at the store, and I rolled my eyes and nodded. The reflection of the silver tool she was using glinted in the overhead lamp. This year she's trying more potatoes. From the cubicle next to us floated some phrases about sheep and a lot of laughter. My hygienist said, "Her daughter's raising a lamb with 4H."

Now we all know that the person who's raising the daughter is also raising that lamb. It made me think of one of my students who wrote a poem once about blow-drying a chicken. It was her daughter's chicken and was going to be shown at the California State Fair.

I know zip about 4H, but I can see that you would want your lamb or rabbit or banty hen to be as beautiful as possible in order to win, so you'd have to bathe it, and apparently an air-dried chicken is not as lovely as a blow-dried one. In my student's poem there was no mention of the time it takes to do this, but I asked. It takes three hours. The chicken likes it, supposedly: sits quietly in your lap, a little sedated by the noise and heat.

This has completely changed my experience of our local county fair. Where **you** might pass through the poultry display considering breeds and coloration, I am seeing mothers and fathers sitting patiently on closed toilet seats all over town, steadying a chicken with one hand, wielding the Conair dryer with the other.

After we laughed and I rinsed out my mouth, my hygienist said she had an African gray goose

that she hadn't been able to find a mate for, and
he'd fallen in love with her instead. This wasn't a
problem until spring rolled around, but now she
can't get anything done because he keeps wrapping
his wings around her leg or trying to climb up on
her back when she's bending over to feed the baby
chicks. "Spring is nuts," she said. "Everyone's
crazy: the goose is after me, the ducks are after the
chickens…"

I smiled back at her with my sparkly teeth. I
knew **exactly** what she was talking about. Driving
home I realized that teeth-cleaning is probably my
version of blow-dried feathers. In any case, I'm
feeling just as happy and crazy this spring as an
African goose.

The Great Crossing

Every autumn we hold a triathlon to honor a local woman who died of cancer and raise money for cancer research. Four hundred women participate, some alone and some in teams, and the mood is vibrant, full of solidarity. The race begins with a half-mile swim from the same boat dock where I launch myself most days all summer to dog-paddle around. In the months beforehand, I see the swimmers training, their seriousness evident in neon bathing caps, goggles, and the beautiful angles their elbows make as they pull themselves through the water, doing the crawl.

I'm envious of those elegant strokes, and intended to learn the crawl last summer. I actually bought goggles, although I've never tried them on. Several friends volunteered to teach me the proper way to breathe. But the fact is, I hate putting my face in the water: I'm afraid to find out what's

down there. My body wants to try that efficient
stroke but my mind is convinced there are sharks,
stingrays, sea monsters and — since my lake is
really a man-made reservoir — probably some
church steeples I don't want to know about. Never
mind the water isn't clear enough to see more than
three feet in any direction.

I prefer to tootle along with my head up, looking
at the beauty around me. There's some mineral in
this water that makes everyone buoyant and I'm
pretty strong, so I'm not afraid I'll tire out and sink.
The osprey diving for fish a few yards away don't
scare me. I just worry about large undocumented
fresh-water octopi grabbing my ankles.

You wouldn't know it looking at me now, but
I was the bow oar in an eight-oared shell on my
college's women's crew, and for a few years we were
undefeated. I'm no longer a Type A personality and
the triathlon doesn't appeal to me, but last summer
I began dreaming about crossing the lake. I've
always had a jones to go somewhere rather than
walk treadmills or swim laps. I like my efforts to
have purpose, otherwise I feel like a hamster. And
this project was the right scale. I was pretty sure I'd
make it, but thought I might need to dig deep for
some willpower near the end. Diana Nyad, I ain't:

the only water I've traversed before is the quarter-mile width of Walden Pond, 20 years ago, and this lake is almost a mile across.

Last year, the "Great Crossing," as my friend Leslie dubbed it, was a huge success, so we did it again on Sunday: 13 swimmers, five boats, and 20 helium balloons to keep us visible and safe from being run over by motor boats. I'm traditionally last, which is sort of charming, and this year I did not need a three-hour nap to recover. It was wonderful: the water was a perfect 82 degrees, and amazingly enough, no one stubbed her toe on a weather-vane or was bitten by a giant snapping lake turtle.

Sniffing Around

Last week I did a lot of driving. I left my house at noon on Friday and whizzed down Interstate 80 toward Santa Rosa, where I had a radio interview to record. After two hours I turned onto Route 12, one of those windy little roads that passes through vineyards and open fields before it enters a crowded necklace of towns, Sonoma and Glen Ellen among them. Just before Sonoma there's a straightaway where someone planted 20 eucalyptus trees in the last century as a wind break. The sudden pungent smell wafting in my windows threw me back to childhood and the drives my family took to visit friends in these rolling hills. Something about heat-soaked eucalyptus bark overlaid with a slight salty note from fog coming in off the Pacific is absolutely unmistakable. Marcel Proust had his famous madeleines, the fluted French cookie whose flavor and texture catapulted him into his past. For me, taste is evocative, but scent is the sense most closely tied to my memory.

Being a Friday afternoon, there was more traffic than I expected. I don't go out into civilization much and in the rural county where I live I never think about traffic unless there's a roadwork project going on. I ended up being an hour late to the interview, but due to the magic of cell phone reception, I was able to warn my interviewer and this wasn't a problem. I did my recording in one take — something I'm famous for, so it's nice when I can pull it off — and then hopped back in the car, headed down 101 toward Berkeley, where I had a reading that night. In this direction the Friday traffic was coming the other way, so I got to feel just a teensy tiny bit smug. I'm not proud of my character flaws exactly, but I try to enjoy them when they surface, before I have to gather my wits and stuff them back into the over-full closet of my psyche. Retribution didn't strike me down with a flat tire for my smugness, and I made it to San Rafael in record time and onto the Richmond Bridge. Here the salt water smell was much stronger, and laced with fish, kelp, diesel oil from the tankers moored in Richmond, and hot asphalt from the repaving they're doing on the bridge. It reminded me of playing outside at the grammar school I went to, right beside the Bay. I could almost hear the red rubber four-square ball slapping against concrete.

Berkeley has that same foggy coolness and salty smell, but diminished again, being farther from shore, and there's a sharp overlay of roasting coffee. Driving up University the mingled scent of East Indian and Thai food chases your car. The reading was in a caffé (with two effs). It started at 7 and ended at 9:30, during which time I drank two decaf cappucinos and talked to about 40 people, at least 38 of them poets. The room buzzed with caffeinated social energy and the slightly acrid aroma poets give off when they're hoping you're going to notice them, admire their work, and maybe even buy their self-published chapbook. Luckily this smell goes well with acidic coffee top notes. It may even be the reason poets perform so often in cafes.

I was back in my car by 9:45, zooming up Interstate 80 again toward Sacramento. Just before the Carquinez Bridge — which carries you over Carquinez Straits, made famous in Stephen Vincent Benet's poem "American Names" — there's the C&H Sugar factory with its big old-fashioned pink neon sign. If you open your passenger window, as I did, the aroma of burnt sugar will fill your car. Not everyone likes this, but it holds a place in my heart from early morning rowing on the Charles River when I was in college. At 5 a.m. on the Cambridge side, the New England Candy Company's factory made NECCO wafers and the smell was so strong it was still in our hair two hours later when we got back to the boat house.

Two hours after C&H Sugar I am 20 miles from home, singing along to Taj Mahal on the radio and feeling as though my life has just flashed before my nose. I've driven 317 miles and been gone 12 hours. The dry pine-and-cedar scent of the foothills is starting to bloom in my nose, but even that's not enough to keep me from getting sleepy. I pull over for gas and do some jumping jacks beside my car, a sight I hope nobody witnesses. I know you're not supposed to do this, but I lean over and inhale the smell of Arco unleaded, 87 grade. It's horrendous.

Plenty strong enough to keep me awake until I reach upper Newtown Road.

One Plexiglass Rhinoceros

This morning I drove across two rivers and
beneath one moving train to get to the periodontist.
I passed about ten thousand trees, growing in perfect
linear rows, all leafed out now, their blossoms blown
away. Mostly almonds and walnuts. Some prune
plums. I saw quite a few brown-and-white cows, and
one plexiglass rhinoceros, to whom I always wave. It
lives in someone's front yard, pretending to be art.

The strawberry fields were open for buying,
even at 7 a.m., and I could feel the heat building as
I got closer to sea level. I descend 2,454 feet, over
about 40 miles, to get my teeth cleaned. This is not
an urban lifestyle. I wouldn't say it's the reason
I left cities, exactly — I had great dental care in
Cambridge, Chicago, and San Francisco. But it's
kind of a weird perk of the rural life, that services
you need are sometimes far-flung, so routine
errands turn into adventures.

My actual dentists, a husband-and-wife team, are right downtown, ten minutes from my house. But a few years ago I had a tooth pulled, and began these treks to Yuba City to see the most wonderful periodontist on earth. Now, twice a year, I get up in the dark and zip down there for an hour's cleaning. Another tooth needs to come out and we've been waiting to decide exactly when. Today I got the news that sooner is better than later, and was sternly advised not to eat any Milk Duds. I'm pretty famous for eating everything but the kitchen sink, but I'm not sure I've had a Milk Dud since 1976.

The two rivers I drove over are swollen with spring run-off, blue and sparkling. I wanted to stop the car and jump in, but knew I would frostbite my toes. The train, like all trains these days, looked old-fashioned: the cars faded into beautiful muted colors, a little rust. And the trestle I was driving under seemed of the same vintage, its lacy metal sides like something out of a movie, not a real crossing and me in a 12-year-old green Toyota.

I'm afraid, despite using a laptop and cell phone all day, every day, I'm feeling a longing for the old-fashioned. A desperate kind of nostalgia has caught me and won't let go. This year, the

speed of life seems radically changed. Just in the
four months we've gone through, so many difficult
things have happened that it's hard to figure
out how to proceed. From the broadest brush
strokes of flood, earthquake, tornado, tsunami,
and radiation leak to the most close to my heart:
a dear friend dying, the world is rocking me.
Not to mention political cruelty and economic
vertigo. I know I'm not the only one who feels
this. Something about spring both brings me
back to a calm center, and amps up my worry.
The recurrence of springs, abundant, green and
cheerful, year after year, is reassuring. But I
also wonder if I'll ever see another: my father
died when he was my age. Either something will
happen to me, or the world will change so fast that
next year spring won't come.

    I try to use road trips like this to settle my
nervous system. I look around and take deep
breaths. I say, "Molly, this is Thursday. Can you let it
just be Thursday?" Even though this month Prince
William of England turned British citizen Kate
Middleton into princess and duchess in the same
breath, and days later someone killed Osama bin
Laden with two shots to the head, the almond meats
on these trees are slowly growing into their secret

oval shapes. Despite gas and food prices soaring
and me needing a tooth pulled out, which will cost
$964 that I don't currently possess, the dogwoods
along Route 20 — graceful, serene as duchesses —
have quietly, overnight, turned princess-pink and
wedding-dress-white.

Training to Watch the Olympics

Don't look now, but the Summer Olympics start tomorrow. I've been trying to get in better shape before they begin. This is partly in solidarity — all those athletes have worked for years to get as good as they are; it seems only right to walk an extra mile in their honor. And it's partly in anticipation of the Sports-watching Couch-potato Injury problem. You know, the way audience members strain and twitch on the sofa so the diver on the screen will make her flips in time to hit the water cleanly? I don't want to inadvertently pull a muscle egging on some fourth-place Latvian discus thrower.

The Olympics are the only reason I wish I still owned a television. Everything else I handle with Oscar parties, HBO rentals, or Downton Abbey Sunday dinners. I watch the British Open and Red Sox games at local bars. But for the Olympics I want to be near a TV all day long. I'm addicted to the intensity, the beautiful bodies doing such hard work, the joy, the youth, and how long these people have worked to get here. I also have a secret Princess Kate fixation, and since this year London's the host, I'm going to be even more glued to the screen, hoping for a glimpse of white teeth, brown hair, and surrealistic head gear.

I'm a good California progressive who can't bear either mainstream advertising or American jingoism, but during the Games I'm able to block all that nonsense out (or judiciously use the mute button). The Olympics were always meant to be outside time, and that's how I treat them. A special couple of weeks, where my politics and common sense get suspended in honor of athleticism, stamina, drive, collegiality, and Speedos.

If you're under 40, you're wondering why the heck I don't watch the festivities on my computer. After all, NBC is live streaming every single event. I'm not sure what to tell you, except I don't know precisely what live streaming is or how to access it, and I don't want to sit at my desk for fun when I have to sit there for work. Yes, I have a laptop. But its screen is too small to show why the judges marked down that Korean gymnast. And don't even start about smart phones. What the younger

generations fail to realize is that Baby Boomers
are all half-blind: we can't see a thing on those tiny
machines, even though we carry them around with
knowing looks and much savoir faire.

Where are YOU watching the Olympics? Maybe
I should come over to your house. I make a mean
cup of Darjeeling, if you're imitating the Brits, and
a meaner Margarita, if you're rooting for Mexico.
I could bring Guatemalan coffee, Greek olives, a
French baguette and baba ganoush.

Because you know we're going to have to do
some carbo-loading to keep up our strength...

FALL

Lingonberries

After keeping my nose to the grindstone for a week and a half, today I tried to take the day off, and failed miserably. Why is it so hard to do nothing? I started out fine. I slept late, did **not** make the bed, and then went out with a friend for breakfast around 11. We snuck over to IHOP hoping no one would see us.

I don't usually veer this far toward middle-American dining, but IHOP is the only place in the U.S. outside Minnesota and IKEA where you can get lingonberries, and I had a craving. If you've never had lingonberries, you're in for a treat. They're a tart little bright red berry, about one-third the diameter of a cranberry, and they grow in Scandinavia. IHOP serves them on thin pancakes and calls them Swedish, but I used to eat them on salty crackers with Jarlsberg cheese when I lived in Norway. They were a godsend at those long

smorgasbord tables when everything else seemed
to be made of herring. The Norwegians should win
a prize, or at least get on Saturday Night Live, for
all the uses they find for herring. And it's quite
revolting, unless you happen to like the flavor of
metal filings marinated in oil and sour cream.

After the lingonberry fix I did some excellent
dawdling — drove around town with my friend
so he could run a few errands, exclaimed over the
brilliant red leaves still on the maples even though
it's been raining all week. But there must have
been some righteous hard-working Lutheran juju
in those lingonberries, because after only an hour
of dawdling, I stopped at my bank and made a
deposit.

This is the way it begins; you do something in
all innocence in the middle of your day off and next
thing you know you're on that slippery slope toward
being productive. I thought I could handle it, of
course. I thought one errand wouldn't hurt, that I
could stop whenever I wanted to, go back to abject
sloth and peace of mind without any ill effect, but
boy was I wrong. A five-minute trip to the bank was
only the beginning. Next thing I knew there was
laundry in the washer, a clean kitchen sink, and I
was at my desk, installing some software I couldn't

get to last week, answering business e-mails,
designing a new promotional bookmark for one of
my classes.

I didn't want to be working — I felt sheepish,
guilty, and deep-down really ashamed — but I just
couldn't help it, I was powerless to stop myself.
Finally one of the cats managed to shut down the
computer by walking on the right combination of
keys with muddy feet and I came to my senses.

Whew! I said to no one in particular. That was
close. I didn't even wipe off the keyboard, I just
strolled back up to the house with the cat in my
arms and fed us both a little tunafish right out of
the can. Then we curled up on the sofa together, him
purring, me humming, the sound of cars slishing by
on the wet road outside. I picked up my novel.

Saved again.

Pining for Petrichor

Last Tuesday, fall arrived in my town: "season
of mists and mellow fruitfulness," according to John
Keats. The temperature plummeted from 91 to 68
and most of us were relieved. It's almost Hallowe'en,
after all, and pitch dark by dinnertime.

To prove my fortitude and general machismo, I
went swimming one more time up at the lake, which
is gorgeous now all the boats are gone and flotillas of
coots have arrived. I might have just taken a photo,
but my friend Betsy had her wetsuit on, and gloves,
and a bathing cap, and I couldn't let her go in all
by herself, could I? They don't make wetsuits in
my size, so I had to rely on my personal insulation
system, which worked beautifully in the end. In the
beginning, the water seemed icy and I complained
a lot, which always helps warm a person up. Some
swearing was also heard. But really, the water's not
that bad, and by the time I'd gotten in, muttering

under my breath, to follow Betsy and Rocky, her
dog, it was comfortable and we swam and swam.

I don't know if you remember from your
childhood what it's like the day after the County
Fair, when the carnies dismantle the rides and Job's
Daughters cart all that used frying oil out of their
booth in five-gallon buckets. Or even after a dinner
party, when you're reaching under the sofa to grab
a stray napkin ring and the sink is full of soapy
water that's lost all its heat and most of its bubbles?
Fall seems like that to me: a season of cleaning up
and putting everything away. Tidy piles of firewood
appear next to my neighbors' houses, and all the
summer toys disappear. In a perfect world, I'd be
up on a ladder cleaning out my gutters, but luckily
perfection has never managed to find me, so instead
I'm sitting on the dead dry grass of my so-called
lawn, eating a windfall pear.

When Keats wrote "season of mists," he was
in England, where it had been raining all summer
long. Here in the globally-warmed Sierra foothills of
Northern California, we don't see rain between early
May and late October. If something looks like mist,
don't hesitate to call 911: it's likely to be the initial
few minutes of a terrible forest fire. The surface
of Scotts Flat Lake, which is really a reservoir, has

dropped 20 feet since the day we first dove in. Some evaporated, but most if it was released downstream to farmers and our town's water treatment plant.

Even though the nights have cooled and the sun's less fierce, everything is still parched: Jeffreys, lodgepoles, manzanita, the golden California grasses, all the small animals and birds. And us big mammals, too: mountain lions, brown bears, and middle-aged former redheads; by this time of year we're longing and pining and waiting impatiently for "petrichor," that incredible smell when hot dry dirt is drenched by the first rain.

It's Only Money

One of these days, I'm going to finally figure out money. You'd think at my age I would have gotten a handle on it. But somehow, despite paying, or not paying, my own bills since I was 20, I've managed to keep money a mystery to myself. Its growth and shrinkage don't seem to be related to anything in the real world, and the things I trade it for don't always make much sense.

Somehow the emotional charge on money takes away my capacity for logic. If I were dealing with, say, blue kitchen sponges instead of federal currency, I think I'd have an easier time. It would be unwieldy: paying the mortgage would require renting a U-Haul truck once a month, but if it would help dispel the fog in my brain, I'd do it. I have no emotional charge related to kitchen sponges. I like the fact that they're blue, but that's the extent of it. I don't feel an impulse to hoard them, or wish

I had just a few more around the house. I don't wake panicked in the night thinking I'll never have enough of them. They're. Sponges. End of story.

American life is not helpful in demystifying money. Credit waltzes around disguised as money to spend, but in reality makes things twice as costly. ATM machines report a different balance than the one you really have in your account because of what's called "float." Prices — real estate, gasoline, the fish of the day — rise and fall when you're not keeping track of them. And there's the cacophony of monetary jargon: puts, calls, margin, overnight foreign exchange rates, pork belly futures options trading... I went to business school to try to figure out what it all meant, and retained my understanding for exactly one hour past the final exams.

Emotionally, money means so much in our culture. Having it is good, but too much makes people jealous. Not having any erases you from the world. The unacknowledged punishment meted out to poor people, blaming them for their condition, is one of the huge social crimes of the last five centuries. I'm sick of it. I want to see money as what it is: a means of trade, not a four-leaf clover or a moral yardstick.

To simplify the whole business, I'm paying for everything with cash this month. It's just paper and mostly green ink, plus germs from other people's fingers. Since it's me, the color-junkie, I'll be choosing purple five-dollar bills over the old green ones, and trying to get red tens when I go to the bank. One wouldn't want to lead a boring life, after all. But gas, groceries, the propane bill — I'll be carrying Ben, Andrew, George, and Abe around in my pocket to trade for what I need.

Four men's names like that in a list, with George among them, makes me think of the Beatles. And that, of course, makes me think of a song. *Can't buy me lo-ove...*

Stockholm Syndrome

So here's the story. Last week I went out to
dinner with some good friends. During the course
of the meal, I said that an organization where I
volunteer was going to have a sexual harassment
training. The man I was sitting beside also
volunteers there, and without missing a beat he
said, "I've **always** wanted to get sexually harassed,
but no one ever chooses me!"

Now, this is a stupid thing to say. Anyone who
thinks it would be fun to get sexually harassed
a) has probably never experienced any kind of
harassment, and b) is probably not a woman.
Because women know the score about sexual
harassment. It was also a fairly hard thing for me
to hear, since I was raped as a child, and rape is
harassment in its extreme form.

The guy, like many guys before him, was
responding to the word *sexual*, and discounting the

word *harassment* — making a kind of guy-like joke
out of the thing. A different kind of man might have
asked why we needed the training, or engaged me in
talking about it more seriously.

What's interesting to me, though, is not his
reaction, but mine. I didn't say, "Shut up, you
bozo" in a friendly tone of voice. I didn't get
ticked off and give him the double-barrel-feminist-
shotgun response, explaining, with dripping
sarcasm, how offensive it was for him to say this,
not to mention unkind. I didn't admit that I was
one of the women who had spent almost a year
organizing the training.

I did this really weird thing: I laughed loudly
and played along. I patted him on his knee and said
in a sexy voice that if he ever wanted some sexual
harassment he should just let me know. Even as
I was doing this, part of my brain was yelling in
outrage, "Are you **crazy**?!!? What are you doing?
You're supposed to help **stop** asinine reactions like
this, not **foster** them for God's sake!"

It took me three days and one sleepless night
to sort it out. He's a big guy, my friend, and he was
crowded in next to me in a booth. I wouldn't have
been able to get out if I had wanted to. He has a
big-guy voice. I'd been having a hard day and was

exhausted before we even sat down to eat. I think those factors greased the way so that I slipped into the prudent response of my childhood when a large man said anything, which was to agree, no matter what I thought, so I wouldn't get hurt.

There's a name for this: it's called Stockholm Syndrome, after a Swedish bank robbery in 1973 when hostages were taken. It refers to the allegiance of victims to their perpetrators, when those perps have been in control for long enough and the violence or threat of violence has been great enough — the most famous example being Patty Hearst joining her kidnappers in the Symbionese Liberation Army and calling herself "Tanya." It's prevalent among child-abuse survivors, battered women, and other victims of violent crimes, as well as prisoners of war.

Once I had figured out what was going on, I stopped beating myself up for being a jerk. I'm going to stop beating my friend up for being a jerk, too. People aren't always careful about what they say, unless they've been taught that it matters.

Gentlemen, please consider this story your training in the fact that it matters. It really matters. Don't be a bozo and crack jokes about it.

You Say Tom-AY-to...

I saw a photo today that made me crack up. It shows a sidewalk chalkboard, the kind restaurants sometimes use, which read: "How to cope with the end of tomato season: 1. denial, 2. anger, 3. bargaining, 4. grief, 5.," and, in big red letters, "CANNING!!" Using Elisabeth Kübler-Ross's stages of grief is part of what makes it funny, but the reality of the sentiment is also hilarious. I don't know about you, but everyone in my town right now is harvesting things and canning them, or freezing or drying or pressing, etcetera. It seems every single person in the county has a garden this year, PLUS there are small farms springing up on every street corner, to supply farmer's markets on Saturday, Tuesday morning AND Thursday night. Goat milk is everywhere. When I asked on Facebook what methods people liked for drying pears, of which I have a plenitude, no fewer than four loans of dehydrators were offered me.

During World War II, Americans were encouraged to grow their own food in "Victory Gardens," the idea being that factories and laborers who usually made food could turn their efforts to munitions instead, and the war might more easily be won. Back then, a lot of people grew their food already, or were only half a generation away from having grown it, so it wasn't much of a leap. Nowadays, though, many have forgotten how to do things our grandparents knew cold. I can cook and bake from scratch, having been raised in the hippie era. I regularly make jam and fruit preserves, but I have no idea what to do with vegetables other than freeze them. How to can food using the water-bath method is a mystery to me, and I'm a little nervous about it because I've read so many pioneer novels where people are killed by botulism from poorly-canned food. I love giving home-made edibles for Christmas, but not if they're poisonous.

The other thing I noticed zipping around the net was a wry motto: "Knitting! Not just a hobby, but a post-apocalyptic survival skill..." This made my stomach hurt, touching, as it does, my new deep-seated fear that whatever the cause may be — global warming, the revolution against corporate power, or World War III — we're going to be living very differently ten years from now, or maybe two years from now.

Part of my coping strategy is to put this fear aside, so let's go back to tomatoes. Since I didn't grow any, I'm going to buy them at the farmers market. I'll slow-roast some, which don't get saved but are eaten immediately, and make sauce out of the rest. A friend's coming over to teach me how to can. In the winter, when I open the Mason jars to use the sauce, if I boil it for ten minutes, apparently the botulism toxin is vanquished. I hope it works.

I promise, I'll test this out on myself before I invite you for dinner!

My Medical Adventure

The friend who brought me home from the hospital gave me a hug and went back to her house. Someone had left a bunch of bananas, anchored to a Get-Well helium balloon. Another had done the dishes and stocked up on groceries. Four different people had tried, unsuccessfully, to pill the cat and left little notes about their efforts. Still kind of stunned, I sat on the sofa and looked out the window for two hours, thinking of nothing.

That was three days ago. I'm still in a disembodied state, although I've explained my medical adventure 200 times over the phone. I don't know why I'm so spaced out. Is it the shock of feeling my own mortality? Is it serenity? Nirvana? A delayed reaction to tubes, needles, catheters, and anesthesia? I have no idea.

My grandfather died at age 57, of his first heart attack, in a hotel on the shore of Lake Titicaca. My

father died at 56 of his fourth, in the old Ghirardelli
Square theater in San Francisco. So when I felt
the proverbial chest pains and electrical sensations
radiate down my shoulder blades and both biceps,
I thought: "Oh, wow, textbook case!" Except it was
all so mild I could hardly believe it had happened.
I even went out to dinner, but then Paula, who's
a nurse and into whose answering machine I had
described the symptoms in amazement, came over
and dragged me off to the ER.

It wasn't a heart attack, it was a potassium
deficiency — hence the bananas. As I understand it,
which is extremely vaguely, potassium helps conduct
electricity in the body, so if you're low, things can
get wonky with your heart, which relies on electrical
impulses to keep beating. You can even die. So eat
your bananas.

I spent the first night in my cozy local hospital,
mainlining potassium. It then seemed logical, given
family history, that I have an angiogram, which is a
fairly science-fictional procedure: they send a little
camera up through your body from hip to heart and
look at the walls of your arteries. For this I went
to an urban hospital famous for cardiology. All I
really remember is that they were playing Santana's
Abraxas in the operating room.

When the little camera finds arterial blockage, which it did, somehow a balloon appears and pooches the blockage out of the way, and then they prop your artery open with a tiny bit of chicken wire called a "stent." Not "stint" — that's how long you're in the hospital. And not "stunt" — that's the procedure itself. S-T-E-N-T, stent. A word with no antecedent.

After all this you're sent home with expensive prescriptions and end up curled on the sofa, watching leaves fall off the trees. Once the incision heals and my body recovers from this ultimately lucky invasion, I'm told improved blood flow and higher potassium will catapult me back into my life.

I hope so. I feel incredibly grateful, don't get me wrong. But all this staring out the window is beginning to worry me.

Poet's Yoga

I just finished a yoga class, led by my friend
Marilyn. I was the only student and we convened on
the floor of her bedroom in San Francisco. She's 68,
slim, and after three years of regular yoga, incredibly
limber: she actually did the splits yesterday, while
showing me how much she's changed, something
she could never do in childhood. We both collapsed in
giggles. I am 51, quite round, and about as flexible as
an I-beam. Nevertheless, I am trying to learn some
yoga because it has increased Marilyn's levels of
serenity and joy so markedly.

In Nevada City, I take classes at a local studio.
There are several postures I'm naturally good at:
lying flat on my back with my eyes closed at the end
of the class is one (that's Yoga Nidra). Sitting with
my knees open and the soles of my feet together
as in prayer is another (Butterfly). Every other
posture, however, is generally beyond me. When

the class is doing Downward Dog, I am doing
Dying Garter Snake. While everyone else rests in
Child's Pose, I'm trying to figure out how to move
my stomach out of the way so the pressure of lying
directly on it doesn't inspire me to invent a new
posture called Barfing Poet. I can't sit cross-legged
without a pillow. My knees don't **want** to be drawn
to my chest, and they certainly don't want to stay
there. Through a complex system of straps and
blocks I can accomplish it, but I feel like Sir Francis
Drake's war horse being lifted off the dock and
lowered into the hold of his waiting ship: helpless
and ridiculous.

I've been doing yoga so infrequently, like once
every three weeks, that there's no accumulation of
flexibility. But I persevere, and this is why: yoga is
teaching me to breathe. Even as my mind reports
that I'm not doing it right, even though I can't
differentiate between the lower part of my lung and
the upper and my inhalations last a nanosecond at
best, I am breathing in and out on purpose, and that
has changed everything.

I have no idea why this is true. Maybe slowing
down enough to do any routine thing on purpose
puts us in a state of awareness that calms us down.
We can't worry about the kids or the mortgage when

we're trying to push out the last ounce of breath with our abdominal muscles. Or maybe the general breathing we do here in America is so shallow and high in the chest, constricting blood flow to the brain, that when we take air deeper into our lungs the oxygen has an immediate beneficial effect.

Whatever it is, I'm grateful. I take this yoga breathing with me now: I practice at stop lights, in line at the bank. I take a few deep breaths when I get into bed, to remind my body to keep breathing this way as I sleep. Deep, slow, measured breathing helps me feel like myself. It makes me laugh more, and already I feel more joy and serenity.

And maybe by the time I get to be 68 I'll be able to do the splits, too.

Requiem

This week most of Southern California's on fire, but it was last week that my sister's house burned down. She's not in the path of those hot Santa Ana winds, she lives in southern Oregon where the rainy season has started, and it's been cold enough to light fires in the wood stove.

Luckily, no one was hurt. Sarah, who's lived in the house for more than ten years, was away, and her boyfriend Paul — the person who cut down the trees, milled the lumber, built the house all by himself, and had cherished it for a quarter-century — was on the Rogue River where he works this time of year as a fishing guide.

Probably the fire started in the chimney. Paul is one of those people who takes fervent care of his possessions, and he cleaned the chimney religiously. I can't tell you how worried it makes me about my **own** chimney to know that **his** can catch fire.

This was one of those houses realtors call a "jewel box." Big enough to be comfortable, lovely proportions, beautiful wooden paneling. Everything made with an eye to craftsmanship and exquisite detail but very livable. A little office for Sarah's business and another for Paul's jewelry-making. An attached greenhouse for passive solar heat and all their plants. A freezer in the laundry room for the fish they like to smoke. We had a wonderful Thanksgiving there two years ago: pouring rain, turkey in the oven, and our niece running around pretending to be a waitress.

My sister and her boyfriend lost everything they owned, except what she had in her suitcase and his boats, safe in a shed out of the fire's range. You don't really think about what "everything" means until you lose it. Her favorite boots, a painting by our aunt, the photos of circus elephants from her college thesis. His fishing rods and guitars. The Windsor dining room chairs she inherited from Mom that all of us wanted. The family silver we grew up setting tables with. Every single thing you can name brings a flood of associations. Those forks lifting blackberry pie to our father's mouth the time he made it and forgot the sugar. Sarah and I and our brother Peter next to each other in those chairs doing homework while Sam played on the floor and our mother paid the bills across the table.

My sister has a kind of resilience that I think is rare, a natural buoyancy and goofy joy that not everyone can muster. She'll probably be in shock for months to come, and I'm not sure she'll ever feel blithe about leaving her house again, even just to run to the market. But already, among the long stretches of sorrow and despair, she's noticing little miracles. A pair of pants she donated to the thrift store this summer still hanging on the rack, and the cashier giving them back to her. The apple-green saucepan that was her favorite, in what used to be the kitchen — stove melted, shelves and counters gone — just sitting there under the open sky, sooty but cheerful, for some incomprehensible reason spared.

Weed-Whacking, the Anti-Depressant

Two teenage boys are making a huge racket
weed whacking my back yard. I wouldn't go so far
as to say this din is an aphrodisiac, but it's definitely
an anti-depressant. In three hours, the two of them,
one six-foot-five and one five-foot-six, both sixteen,
have done everything on my to-do list except plant
zinnias, and I want to do that myself. I'm feeling
grateful, delighted, relieved, and did I say grateful?
Incredibly grateful. I'm quite sure that actual
lines on my forehead are disappearing as the grass
succumbs to their machines. Their parents would
probably disagree, but for me, these kids are human
Botox.

One thing about living alone is it's hard to do
everything that needs to be done all by yourself. It's
possible. I've done it. But it's not that much fun.
It's a burden on your mind before you do it, and
then doing it is usually dusty, hot, grubby, prickly,

annoying, and takes a long time. When you're finished, all you can think about is what's next on the list. *How tall is the grass? Has fire season started yet? Do I have defensible space? Did my weed-whacker die over the winter? Do I have any of those little bottles of oil you're supposed to add to the gas?* I don't mean to sound like either a city slicker or a helpless female, I'm just letting you read the ticker tape machine in my head. In the winter time, my mental burden is firewood, although there's some overlap, because if you're smart, you'll get your wood in during June, when it's cheaper. I am occasionally smart, but more often I am buying it in October for top dollar and stacking it in the rain.

There is only one of me, and I have a lot of resistance to getting chores done. Luckily, God invented teen-age boys and once in a while, they're willing to work for money. They have strong backs for lifting heavy flower pots, long arms for reaching to clip wisteria that's trying to winkle its way under the roof shingles, and require only water to keep going for hours. Well, water and praise, and a drive home afterward, and a very reasonable hourly rate, in cash please. Today we stopped at the corner store to get the right change so each of them could be paid the same amount,

and they immediately bought ice cream bars
with their earnings. The other great thing about
teenage boys is watching them eat. It's like having
your own small herd of ravenous wildebeests.

I came home to a very quiet house. Four out
of five cats were sacked out on the bed, exhausted
from all the disturbance. One sprawled on my desk,
waiting for me to sit down again and keep him
company while he slept. It was eerily quiet, but
then a whistling bug piped up, a few birds began to
argue, and the wind swept through and rang all my
neighbor's chimes.

Home-Made Grape Juice

For the seventh year in a row, I did not enter my plum jam in the County Fair. I watched the deadline approach and then waved when it went past. Partly this comes from being caught up in the usual hustle and bustle — who has time to fill out one more form? And partly it's because not much was ready to pick in early August, when the Fair entries are due. Everything ripened late this year because of a cold wet May, and now, of course, it seems to all be happening at once. There are still peaches in the farmer's markets, next to the pumpkins, and **strawberries,** of all things — even a few plums are still on the trees. A friend of mine who runs a restaurant went picking at a secret location with some of her staff and brought me back her overflow of an amazing pink seedless grape, to the tune of twenty pounds or so.

My kitchen, which was spotless for two days due to my procrastinating about something else, is

now full of big plastic storage containers of grapes,
colanders separating pulp from juice, the Cuisinart
with which I pulverized the plum skins to an edible
size, water baths on the stove boiling jars and lids,
and some open bottles of zinfandel, which I add
to everything. My four now-teenage kittens have
learned to play soccer with strawberries bobbing
in the sink as well as grapes that have leapt onto
the floor, and there are sticky pawprints on every
conceivable surface.

I can't tell you how happy this makes me. One
of the things I miss from my upbringing is the
chaos we could get up to in my parents' kitchen
cooking together. My friend Peggy and I would pick
blackberries all over town and then make jam and
pies, or we'd go after plums in our and our neighbors'
yards and my mother would make Chinese plum
sauce. Just the idea of people doing huge messy
kitchen projects that will result in something, whether
it's temporary, like dinner, or lasting, like 30 jars of
jam to give away for Xmas, makes me feel as though
everything's right with the world.

Everything, of course, isn't really right with
the world. What might become of us is up in the air
and I think that understanding permeates almost
everyone's thoughts in some way, together with

confusion about what to do about it. A friend just wrote a poem about the BP Oil Spill and included a line referencing the day it started, April 10, 2010: "If this was the end of the world as we knew it, we didn't know it." Maybe the end of the world has already started. I, for one, can't tell. And maybe my jam-making frenzy is a futile effort to try to be safe when there's no way to be safe. I might put up enough jam this week for two years worth of peanut butter sandwiches, but knowing how to preserve fruit isn't going to do me any good when we're out of water, much less jars, lids, sugar and Sure-Jell.

What's going to do me the most good regarding an uncertain future is curiosity, love of living, and a respect for my own capacity to change. Which is why I'm boiling an insane number of grapes on the stove this morning.

I've never made grape juice before. Have you?

Reality, What a Concept!

Last week I had a tooth extracted, fell down
and reamed my left leg while I was rescuing a cat,
and lost a friend to melanoma. Mercury is going
to be retrograde for 16 more days. If you don't
live in California, let me just say this is not good
news. When Mercury is retrograde, according to
the astrologists among us, things you've never even
imagined go wrong.

The tooth had been root-canalled since my
senior year of college, but it still hurt to get it
out, and the really fun part was throwing up over
the deck railing all night when I turned out to be
allergic to Vicodin. The leg went through its storm-
to-sunset-to-slime-mold color progression and then
cleared up, except for a red patch on my shin where
blood doesn't seem to be reabsorbing very well.
Apparently this can be dangerous, so I've spent the
last four days on the sofa with my leg propped above

my heart, alternately working on my laptop and reading thrillers.

I used to read novels all the time, five or six a week. Reading was how I relaxed, traveled, dispelled loneliness, and distracted myself from the real world's annoyances and obfuscations. About three years ago, right around when I got on Facebook and also began a tumultuous relationship, I stopped. There was too much else going on, and I was getting so much social contact from the computer and the boyfriend, I didn't need to dip into the lives of fictional people to feel as if I was part of an interesting larger world. The boyfriend is now history, and Facebook has become kind of routine, but I hadn't picked up a novel until this leg business put me on the sofa.

I think my willing suspension of disbelief has a crack in it. Granted, I'm reading thrillers, which are unlikely to begin with. But at least half my brain is commenting as I read, and the remarks are not kind. "Oh, are you kidding? That makes no sense. Right, how convenient! Next thing you know some lovely, long-legged woman is going to come on the scene — see? Like clockwork. Spare me..." Usually I have no trouble throwing books across the room if they're idiotic, and I've done so with quite a few authors. But the thrillers I'm reading this week are by people whose work I always liked before.

Some of this is having stepped away for so long: the plot twists are too obvious, the characters too shallow and predictable. When you read a lot, you get to kind of liking fictional people despite these flaws, but I haven't built up the requisite patience with them yet. And some of this is because my friend Rodger just died.

When real death enters your immediate vicinity — when you watch the flesh at someone's temples turn porcelain white and sink in toward the skull, making beautiful but terminal hollows — then the superficiality of fictional death seems absurd. Someone in a thriller gets shot and is left lying on the floor while the plot races on without him. One of your friends reaches his last week with cancer and you watch his wife and daughters getting used to the idea. You think of what you could say that might be meaningful. The world slows down and takes on more intense colors. My sense of smell actually got a whole lot better in Rodger's last days.

Fiction isn't going anywhere, and I'll probably shift from thrillers to classics, to cut out some of the ridiculousness. But I think I've crossed a threshold, where reality is more appealing than it used to be. There's something about it that's just... I don't know... REAL. That matters. I'm not sure I have time for things that don't.

Maybe I've finally bumped up against my own mortality.

Where There's a Will

Well, at last I did it — I made the appointment with an estate lawyer to draw up my will. You know what this means, don't you? It means some day I'm going to die. Most people avoid making wills for this very reason, and until today I've been one of them. I don't know if it's superstition or intuition that tells us if we **admit** we possibly **could** die, then Death will find out and come knocking. This is magical thinking at its finest — a four-year-old's general perspective — but that doesn't stop us. The other way to say it is: "If I don't make a will, then maybe I won't die, because I'm certainly not **ready**!" It is so absurd, yet I can feel all my brain cells nodding in agreement.

I, of all people, should know better. My very own father died at the movies, totally unready. He had not made a will. He hadn't even done the dishes. Aside from his "personal effects," which means clothes, books, pots and pans, furniture, and car, everything he owned would have become the property of the State of California, except luckily he was pretty much insolvent so they didn't get anything but credit-card debt, which they ignored. If I were to die intestate, California would get a lot of poetry books, some geraniums, and many wonderful cats.

Let's hope that doesn't happen. Instead, I'm going to try to figure out what things to leave to whom. You parents have an easy out here, you can just say, "divide equally among the children." Lacking kids, I have to think further. I've got two nieces, one nephew, two real godsons and two honorary ones, three siblings, a current sister-in-law and a former, nine first cousins, nine second cousins, and two aunts (with wonderful husbands). That's 34 people. Counting them makes me dizzy and I haven't even started enumerating my friends. I wish I had lots of money to leave, it would be so much fun. But at the moment, I don't. I have books I'm not sure they'd read, clothes that won't fit them, a few family mementoes with huge sentimental value to me, a late-'90s green Toyota, and a riding lawn mower. What else? Flower pots, my college thesis, some very nice ten-year-old Ralph Lauren sheets.

Making a will, in my case, is like holding a yard sale and forcing customers to take specific things home with them. And I keep forgetting I'll be dead! When I say to myself, "I think Sarah would like those pearl earrings," or "Sam should have the painting of Vermont," a voice in my head pipes up at once and says "Hey! I **like** those earrings, why does Sarah get to have them?!?" and "That's **my** painting of Vermont!" The whole thing is ridiculous. And so unnecessary, really, since I have no intention of dying.

But just to make sure, I should probably cancel that appointment with the lawyer, don't you think?

WINTER

Sentimental Value

Today I went to my mother's house for the final
time. She's been dead for six years, four months,
and three days, not that I'm counting. When she
died we were bereaved and unorganized, and left a
lot of her stuff — the things we didn't immediately
want or have to deal with — in the garage, the
attic, the linen closet. . . and one of my brothers
moved in on top of it all. Now that it's time to sell
the house and my brother has moved out, the rest
of us congregated one last time — partly to sort
things and claim any Tupperware containers or
mismatched linen napkins we might want, and
partly to say goodbye.

I devoutly wish we had dealt with this junk six
years ago. When I got there, the house looked like
a bomb had gone off, scattering papers, pot lids,
and hand towels in every direction. Some of it was
anonymous, and therefore disposable, but there

were dangerous pitfalls. It's amazing what happens to middle-aged persons suddenly faced with the pale green wash cloth they used in childhood, little black penguins still marching across its hem. Objects I could not have dredged from my memory at gun point suddenly matter more to me than my left arm.

Try to dissuade your parents from dying. You are not yet old enough to deal with the family face cloths. You are never going to be old enough. To be fair, my mother died on the youngish side, and by the time she realized the chemo wasn't working, she didn't have energy left to purge the garage. Many parents are able to do several rounds of divestiture, so by the time you have to cope with odds and ends, most of them have already been sent to a third-world nation by the Goodwill.

I took some things, here and there: a battered silver bowl that none of us had ever seen before, fabric my mother had never cut or sewn. Some things I bade goodbye to: the penguin face cloth, which was shredding at one end and would have looked ridiculous framed on my wall. The plum tree my mother had loved, and the views out three of her windows at nearby wooded hills. I made my farewell to the frayed purple ribbon attached to the overhead light's pull cord above the washing machine. I tied that ribbon up there when I was 28, so my 5-foot-3-inch mother would stop risking her neck climbing an unsteady ladder to reach it.

The thing about memory is that it doesn't mean anything to anyone but you. It's almost lonely, if you think about it. My siblings don't react to the same things I do, and likewise they have relationships with stuff in that house that I know nothing about.

It's not a fancy house, and the layout is peculiar, so the new owners will probably tear it down and build on the footprint. Maybe they'll rip out the plum tree, who knows? The pull cord and its ribbon, hanging down in front of the washing machine, will definitely be history.

Except when, every once in a while, I remember them.

Art

I've just spent the last two weeks traveling on
the East Coast, seeing relatives and friends and
sitting on a panel at a writers' conference. Despite
circulating like fish in a tank with 7000 writers in
the New York Hilton for three days, when I look
back on the trip what I remember isn't language
but art. My Aunt Mary's new paintings of the salt
marsh out her studio window that are so literal and
dreamlike at the same time. My cousin Miranda's
enormous portrait-in-progress of one of her sons.
My retinas are holding fast to the drawings from
Florence's Uffizi Gallery that I saw in New York,
and those classic renderings jostle for attention
with disturbing antebellum Southern scenes done in
silhouette by the young black artist Kara Walker.

What amazes me is how much art can say without
words — how much emotion one image can evoke.
And while the written word builds its argument in

layers — think of the Gettysburg Address, say, or a poem you recall from childhood — a painting comes to you all at once. That completeness is incredibly potent — an onslaught instead of a gathering. You do look at images and notice more detail over time, but you can't start that way, just examining a hand in the lower left corner. You have to take in the whole thing first. I envy that initial wallop more than I can say, for how immediately it captures the viewer and slips in underneath the mind, directly into the blood.

I'm sure there's more to say about how art works, but I'll leave that to my famous uncle, John Updike, who's known for his art criticism as well as his fiction. His smiling face was among Irving Penn's portraits of artists and writers at the Morgan Library, and I was immediately awash in nostalgia to see it: John aged about 38, hair still brown, with his iconic nose and big teeth. Each writer there — Philip Roth, Norman Mailer — had a hand near his face, as if Penn had asked them to include their instrument in the photo.

A few days earlier I stood on a porch north of Boston where my sculptor cousin Michael, John's son, was carving a marble headstone. His girlfriend recently died of cancer. It was snowing, the flakes mixing with marble dust on the table, the stone half

block, where it wasn't worked on, and half scrolled
top and twining ivy, with a dove perched at one
corner and the woman's chiseled name. Michael
designed it to fit in with the other stones in the New
England graveyard where she lies — same typeface
for the letters, same granite plinth. Now I can't stop
thinking about art and its relation to devotion —
what it's like to use your skill and your craft in an
act of love.

A big part of art's history, of course, is
expressing a devotion to God. Maybe that's why it
moves me so much. Even though I'm never sure
about God's existence, I've always believed in love.

Meeting Your Reincarnation

During my twenties, I was good friends with an elderly woman named Margit Bensen. Margit had been a midwife in her hometown of Ytterstad, Norway, population 35. She emigrated here in 1922, ending up in Boston, and was eventually able to find work as a lady's maid. A few years later, she met Aarne Bensen, a Norwegian bricklayer, and married him.

When I met Margit, in my senior year of college, she was 76 and I was 21. She worked at the Harvard Biology labs, sterilizing the glassware that scientists and grad students used for their experimenting in a huge centrifuge. She wore enormous gloves made of some heat-resistant material, and, with silver braids pinned up on her head, looked angelic and demonic in about the same proportion. My boyfriend was studying mushrooms, and he kept telling me I had to meet his friend Margit. He was so insistent

I thought it was weird, especially when he told me how old she was, but when I finally agreed, Margit and I fell in love at first sight. Not romantic love. We instantly had that mysterious connection you get with some people — we recognized each other. We also looked eerily alike. It sometimes felt as though she had been reincarnated early, in me, and was getting the rare experience of meeting herself the next time around.

My boyfriend went off to medical school and married the next woman he found, and I spent a decade seeing Margit once a week. She taught me Norwegian and we mixed it with English back and forth in a random pattern, so pretty much no one else could understand us. I lived in Norway after college, and then came back and told her stories about her family, whom I had visited way above the Arctic Circle in the Lofoten Islands.

Margit had hundreds of friends and was in touch with most of the grad students who'd passed through her lab, but she and Aarne hadn't had children. I ended up standing in as her next generation. She got older, and I balanced her checkbook and took her to doctor appointments. When the time came, we drove around Boston looking at what were then called "old-folks' homes" until she chose the least dreadful one to move to. While downsizing, she gave me her Norwegian-English dictionaries, a small plate that says "smør" (butter in Norwegian), and a bloodstone ring she said she'd "made Aarne buy" for her in 1930.

She died when she was 89 and I was 33. Now that I've ended up not having children either, sometimes I look around and wonder if anyone will appear out of the blue to balance my checkbook. I'm a little young for that still, but maybe I've met her already. Will it be one of my nieces? A friend's kid? Maybe it will be Margit herself again: someone who looks a lot like me and feels so familiar, she might be my reincarnation.

Where the Boys Are

When I was young and single, a friend said to me, "Molly, in order to meet men, you have to go where they are! You know: race tracks, rodeos, ball games, new car showrooms… maybe the trading floor of the Stock Exchange." I looked at her and rolled my eyeballs. First of all, this is rather sexist. And second, the day I go to a new car showroom to meet men has not yet arrived. New cars are not part of my lifestyle. But ever since her suggestion, I've kept an eye on where men congregate, and why.

Recently I've found a new place. At 7 a.m. Monday, Wednesday, and Friday, a bunch of men gather on the second floor of our local hospital, at Cardiac Rehab. There are 14 of them and one of me, which is odds I like. I'm not cruising for a boyfriend, I just prefer **lots** of attention. And I get it! These guys are rowdy, sassy, occasionally profane, and a whole lot of fun. They tease each

other, and me, in between our three ten-minute
sessions on the treadmill and the recumbent
bike, our stretching before and afterwards, and
our meditation. They also tease the staff, four
professional women who write down our statistics,
take our blood pressure, and monitor our hearts
on a computer screen.

I didn't expect to be a member of this group, and
if you'd asked me, I would have said no **way** was I
going to hang out with a bunch of Neanderthals at
this hour of the morning. But life doesn't always go
the way you plan, does it?

Two of my close friends have belonged to
Cardiac Rehab for years, so I'd heard about it before
my own "heart event." They both encouraged me to
join up, so — half for myself, half to please them — I
did. Now I go because I love it. Where else can you
be sure to laugh your head off before eight in the
morning and get a good workout too?

Like any group, the members take on certain
traditional roles. There's the class clown, the loner,
the snappy dresser. There's the one with a sweet
smile and the one who glowers most of the time but
is harmless. I've only known these guys a month,
but already I'm in love with them. I don't know
what kind of heart problems they've had, and we

don't talk much about our outside lives. We spend an hour and a quarter together on our healing.

Cardiac Rehab is a place I feel very safe. I know the medical staff is going to tell me if my heart does a backflip, and the gentlemen are going to tell me if I'm out of line in any other way, so I'm relaxed: I just concentrate on breathing in and out and using my muscles.

I wouldn't want to say it was **worth** having a blocked artery so I could get to meet these jokers, that would be going a little too far. But since I **did** have one, I'm very happy to have fallen in with this particular band of thieves. And my cardiologist approves. Whenever I tell her stories about their antics, my blood pressure drops ten points.

21st Century Women's Group

Last night, for a few minutes, I stood outside a restaurant on the sidewalk in the dark talking to a friend. There had been three of us at dinner, but one had to scamper off and just two of us were left, standing next to my car. It was one of those moments I cherish, the edge of something, the lingering before it ends.

We'd spent a couple of hours together, talking intimately and deeply about what matters to us, and laughing a lot in between the seriousness. None of us were in a crisis, we were just catching up on each other's lives — but not superficially. Not: "my daughter had the flu last week," but "I feel as if I've changed this year and I'm not used to who I am now, what do **you** think?"

I can't tell you how important it is to me to have friends like this. I'm someone who doesn't know what she thinks unless she's talked or written

about it — I work my way into the truth by trying
to describe what's going on. The feedback of my
friends, as well as their love and amazement at my
fabulousness and/or foibles, really helps me feel as
though I exist.

You would think a person with as much wood to
stack as I have would understand that she exists,
but occasionally I just feel as though I might float off
and never be seen again, like a balloon some child
has let go of after the birthday party. It's one reason
stacking wood is good for me, to remind me that I
live inside a body, which can work hard and smell
the cold edges of the air. I am not just a brain full of
ricocheting ideas or uncontained emotions. When
I meet with these friends I get a chance to present
the ideas — every last well-considered or half-baked
one of them — and not float off into the sky. My
friends say, "That sounds good!" or "Are you out of
your **mind**?!" They can help me remember that I
was aiming for something six months ago, and I've
reached it. They can show me how much better I've
gotten at coping with what is hard.

What I haven't told you yet is that these friends
are women, and we call this our women's group.
I guess I'm holding back because that seems like
such a '70s concept, with so many clichéd notions

about it. We do **not** sit around talking about how
obnoxious men are and practice using speculums.
This is the 21st century. We understand that
men aren't demons, and we've known how to use
speculums (specula?) for 30 years.

What we do is help each other be the most
essential versions of ourselves. I want to be the
Molliest Molly that I can discover — under the
layers of good girl, smartypants, never-had-kids, and
child-abuse survivor — and I need help to get there.
I need people to say, "You know, it doesn't seem as
though you really want that," so I can look up from
the daily hysteria and realize, "You're right! Then
what on **earth** am I doing it for?"

Choosing Your Own Community

This month I've gone to two memorial services, both for the mothers of friends, and am just about to deliver some rose petals I've dried to another pal whose daughter is getting married on Sunday. Last month I went to the wedding of my ex-boyfriend's nephew. I'm doing these things because I want to and I love the people involved, but there's more than that going on. As I've driven home from each of these shindigs, I've thought to myself: "This is what you do when you're part of a community." What I mean is: This is what **"I"** do when **"I'm"** part of a community.

The word "community" gets bandied about a lot these days, what with the economic and political collapse going on around us and people starting to imagine post-apocalyptic scenarios. What does it really mean? What does it mean to you? For me, it's a mix of people I know and love, like friends and family, people I maybe don't know so well but see

a lot, like Margot at the grocery store and Alexis at
my favorite coffee shop, and people I don't know
well and rarely see but feel connected to: Peter
Van Zant and Izzy Martin, both former county
supervisors, my M.D. and nurse practitioner, my
dentists, Rex at the car repair place, my vet. Being a
hemi-semi-demi-famous poet in this county, there's
also a circle of people who know me but I don't know
them — they're part of my community all the same.
And then there are trees and birds and animals, the
landscape itself, the South Yuba River.

   The way I see it, all relationships bring with
them a certain responsibility — part of belonging
to a community is deciding for ourselves what that
is. By responsibility I mean envisioning how we'll
fit in, what we'll offer and what we'll take, what we
"owe" our community and what we don't. People
make different choices about this, and I think every
choice is valid. There are hermits who grocery shop
right before closing on Saturday nights, to see as few
strangers as possible. They'd never be caught dead
at the Fourth of July parade. There are political
activists who stand on our overpass dressed in black
on Thursday evenings with placards protesting the
war in Iraq, contributing their political opinions.
There's the person who sits on boards of non-

profits all over town and raises significant money to support them. There's me, trying to decide how to decline the next three benefits I'm asked to read at, just because I've done so many and now I have to get some of my own writing done.

There are people who go to weddings and funerals and people who don't. People who tip well when they eat out and people who don't. Lots of opposites like this, and all gradations in between. There are hospice and library volunteers, firefighters, Search & Rescue. There's the woman who configures my neighborhood association's newsletter and collects our membership fees. We can even include the hat-wearing robber who's hit several banks this year and remains at large. Even if he doesn't live here, he's choosing to be part of our community by stealing our money. And we'll include him, in turn, by locking him into our county jail if we catch him.

One way I support the community is to go to weddings and funerals. Weddings used to make me jealous or cynical, and funerals made me too sad. But I've changed. Maybe it's my age, and a lengthening perspective. Now, something about the generations represented really moves me: there are always at least two and sometimes as many as five.

Families look like each other, which is comforting. I can see time hold still for a second, right in front of my eyes.

Whether grocery trucks cease rumbling up 49 into the Safeway parking lot and we start eating food we grow in our own back yards or not, each of us still has only a very short time here. I think it's worth asking outright how you want to spend yours. If the Fourth of July were in October, I'd go to the parade every year, but most of the time I can't bear the heat. I vote for tipping at least 20 percent because I used to be a waitress: I remember what it's like to smile all night and carry dirty dishes across a hard floor.

Two lines are coming to mind from different poems as I write this. The last of Mary Oliver's "The Summer Day": "What is it you plan to do with your one wild and precious life?" And the end of Kristy Nielsen's "Poem Against Indifference": "So, these are the people you'll die with, these the ones you must love."

Writing to Heal

The day after my mother died of ovarian cancer, I went to my local library to teach a writing class. I thought about canceling, because I was crying at unexpected moments, but the class was for cancer patients, and it felt as though they were the people I should be with that day. I don't remember much about it, frankly, except that we all cried, and we wrote about cancer: what it had taken from us, what it had taught us, and the stupid advice well-meaning people had given us that didn't help. We wrote about our experience. This is not going to surprise any of my students. I'm a literal writer, and I teach that way: I want people to write about what they feel and know and gather up with all their senses. I think if everyone did this we could save the world.

This was an audition, and I got the job. After I was hired, I thought I should find out more about how writing worked in healing. I knew from being a child-abuse survivor that it was helpful, but all the evidence seemed to be anecdotal. Eventually I found the research of James Pennebaker. In his book, *Opening Up: The Healing Power of Expressing Emotions,* Pennebaker describes experiments he did to establish whether or not writing was actually, physically, healing.

The first involved writing for 15 minutes every day for four days. Three groups wrote about the most traumatic thing that ever happened to them, but in different ways: one vented their emotions about the trauma but didn't mention it by name, one wrote about the details of the trauma but not their emotions, and one included both details and venting. The fourth group wrote about what their dorm room looked like. Pennebaker had two months' health service records for his subjects, and tracked them for four months after the experiment. Only one group showed a significant change. The students who wrote about *both* their trauma *and* their emotions cut their health-service attendance in half.

He repeated the experiment, this time drawing blood at several points in the process, and found that not only were the health-service results duplicated, but the T-cell count of participants in that group was elevated for as long as six weeks afterward. Pennebaker concludes that his participants are using both sides of their brains simultaneously: the left, logical brain describing the event and the right, ricocheting brain expressing the emotional reaction.

Needless to say, I don't draw blood from my cancer students. But I designed an exercise that uses both sides of their brains, in order to boost the immune system, and I get them to laugh, cry, and sometimes sing in class, which has got to be good for you. I've been teaching it for thirteen years now, and it feels like excellent work to be doing in the world.

The person who would really be proud, though, if she were here, is my mother.

Birthday Card for My Brother Sam

Tomorrow my younger brother Sam turns 50.
I still don't believe it.

From my vantage point of eldest kid in the
family, Sam still seems about eight years old. Even
at his wedding. Even at our mother's memorial
service. The jaunty eight-year-old grin and blond
hair flopping over his forehead are clearly visible to
me behind the surface of this bearded adult.

I have plenty of friends who are 50 and 40 and
30, and I don't feel much older than they are. We
trade wisdom and understanding back and forth
regardless of our years, the same way I do with my
friends who are 60 and 70 and 80. But I didn't take
any of them to see Fred Astaire movies at the Surf
Theater when I was in high school. They didn't
tap-dance up the aisle singing "Shall We Dance?"
to the applause of a motley San Francisco audience
in 1971. None of them came out with legendary

pronouncements while running to be first into the car on a family outing. For 44 years we've repeated what Sam said, as a way to fend off reality at various moments: "Anyone ahead of me is not in the race!" A Zen koan, out of the mouths of babes, if only we'd known what the heck that was. It's a very smart mantra for the youngest in a competitive and sarcastic family.

Sam is famous for his Christmas-present wrapping ingenuity. One year he gave me a pair of earrings "wrapped," quote unquote, in a banana. He cut two little plugs out of the side, maybe half an inch deep, put one earring into each hole, and then put the plugs back in on top. No paper. No ribbon. Just a browning banana under the tree with a little card taped to it. Not everyone's brother can find something around the house to wrap a present in that is this funny and this effective at the same time. I definitely had no idea what the present was, which is the point of wrapping in the first place.

Last month we got a generalized hate letter here at the station, directed at broadcasters and staff alike. The disparaging remark about me was the name "Molly I-Have-More-Friends-Than-You-Do Fisk." When I heard this, my second thought was, "what's wrong with having a lot of friends?!" But my first thought was, "Hey, you haven't met my brother Sam!"

Sam sees friends from our old neighborhood once a month, and a circle called The 8th Graders meets for drinks several times a year. He and his closest pals are in and out of each others' houses daily. I met these people when they were four feet high, most memorable for making too much noise and each drinking half a gallon of milk at one meal. I'm sure they'll gather around for Sam's birthday tomorrow. They may even drive themselves to his party, though I can't imagine how their feet will reach the pedals.

Molly's Manifesto

Once a year I step back from my life to look at what's going on. I ask myself what the heck I'm doing, and is it working? Am I having fun, making a living, and doing something useful in the world? Is there a new direction I might want to steer in? I think about these things at other times of year, but I don't make decisions until December, to get a leg up on the new year.

I've been a poet for 23 years, and a writing teacher for 18. In the current recession, my business fell off enough that I regrouped and took on additional work. I'm studying to be a Life Coach, specializing in writing, and I consult with small businesses on social media. While rooting through old computer files, I came across a kind of manifesto I'd written several years ago and discovered my new jobs fit very neatly into the picture. Saying things publicly helps me keep myself honest, and I wanted to share with you what I'm about, as poet, teacher, coach, consultant, friend, woman, and human being. Here's Molly's Manifesto:

"I want to help people be more fully themselves, find their core strengths and beliefs and hold to those against the deep distractions of our culture. I think the work of a life is distilling oneself down to the richest possible essence. I want to become the Molliest I can possible be.

In all my work, I want to further the discussion about what is human, about the individualness we each carry, and how we weave ourselves together to form communities. Our individuality is the source of our gifts — what we can contribute to those communities and the larger world. We must explore our own quirks, skills and essential natures, and protect ourselves against the tidal pull of a culture that encourages us to conform to an imagined norm. The force of this culture cannot be underestimated. It's money-based and insatiable. But human life is based on love and connection, not on money.

Our culture asks us to spend a huge amount of time and energy avoiding our gifts. Rather than supporting our trumpet practice, the culture proposes that we buy inessential things — a newer car, more clothing than we can possibly wear out — using our practice time to earn the money for it. We're encouraged to worry about our looks, weight, and sexual desirability rather than learning to build a house or plant a garden. And instead of promoting the empty time necessary for inventing a new poem or painting, we're seduced with so many forms of entertainment that our heads spin.

All these distractions, we are told, will make us happy. This is a lie. What makes humans happy is finding, developing, and sharing our gifts. Mastering what we love to do. Teaching other people how to do it, too.

I want to help people hone their ability to fight the culture and learn to be devoted to the exploration and enhancement of their own gifts, as I am devoted to mine. I want to support us all in this devotion, and, of course, to have a bunch of fun while we're doing it."

Xmas Lights

Well, here we are, only ten shopping days away
from Christmas, and you can feel the hysteria coming
off the K-Mart parking lot in waves. All day, streets
are clotted with traffic, something we don't handle
very well around here. I've had people honk at me
this week, cut me off, rush through stop signs when it
wasn't their turn and glare at me for no reason. I'm
trying not to take it personally. I'm trying to make
it my spiritual practice to not let anyone tick me off.
Christmas, for all that I love the colored lights and
goofy decorations, not to mention the idea of holiness
that it was originally based on, is incredibly hard, and
people need to be cut some slack.

Expectations are terrifyingly high. We grown-
ups wander around in just as much of a haze as
kids do. The kids are thinking, "Oh, will I get that
Star Wars game with the purple thingamajigs?" and
adults are thinking, "Will the toy store have any

of those Star Wars games left? Will I be able not to strangle her if she mentions it one more time!?"

I don't know which is worse: having expectations, or being worried that you won't fulfill somebody else's. I suppose this is the terrain marriage counseling is built on. But at Christmas, it spills over big-time into everyone's lives and we walk around feeling harassed instead of enjoying the rain sluicing down on the colored lights.

I say "Bah, humbug!" to all this angst, and here's what I want you to do. Go to the grocery store and buy half a gallon of eggnog and some powdered nutmeg. Pour it into as many cups as you have family members, or friends if you're doing this with friends. For grown-ups who aren't driving, you can add some rum. For the driver, you can make an eggnog latte. The kids get it straight, with extra nutmeg sprinkled on top.

Now jump in the car. If you know where the good Christmas light displays were last year, head over there. But if you haven't done this before, just explore. Tool around your own neighborhood, and then pass by the houses of your friends and your kids' friends. *Oooh* and *aaah* over the lights you find. Sing every Christmas carol you know. Sing Good King Wenceslas, with the kids taking the part

of the page and the grown-ups the part of the King.
If you're Jewish or Muslim or Buddhist or Hindi or
don't know any carols, sing show-tunes instead, at
the top of your lungs. If you're doing this by yourself
and hate singing, put Handel's Messiah on the CD
player, or Alison Krauss.

It would be nice if we could all gather around the
hearth and roast chestnuts at this time of year, but
let's face it: somebody will be playing video games,
or texting her new boyfriend, or watching TV. Get
your family out of the house and into the car where
they can't escape togetherness. Make them leave the
electronic devices at home.

Christmas light displays are one of the last
remaining true American folk arts, and they deserve
our attention. People risk their lives putting those
reindeer on the roof, for Pete's sake! Let them know
it wasn't in vain.

Word for the Year

Like many of you, I've learned through personal experience that making New Year's resolutions is idiotic. It's such common practice in America, though, I think a little discussion may be in order. And I have an alternative to suggest.

We've all eaten and drunk our way through December, and now it's time for remorse, regrouping, and resolutions. We're going to lose weight, stop smoking, exercise regularly and learn Spanish or Mandarin, all while cutting down on the cocktails and only driving ten miles over the speed limit. There's one big flaw in this logic that no one ever mentions, though, and it's timing. If we were making resolutions on Memorial Day or the 4th of July, our chances of success would skyrocket. Warm weather and blue skies encourage happiness, and happiness encourages success. Trying to improve ourselves in January is just silly. In January, we should be sitting in front of the fire reading books or dozing, like the big mammals we are.

My friend Jane has a better idea of what to do on January 1st: pick a word for the year. This is something you can ruminate on before the fire or curled under your blankets just before you fall asleep. Choosing a word doesn't go against the seasonal requirements of your inner Grizzly.

In my five years of following this practice, the minute I open my mind to find a word, the word finds me instead. And won't go away, even when I want it to. "Surrender" was one from a few years ago that I just hated. I wanted "love" or "kindness," something overtly positive. But "surrender" turned out to be fruitful: I learned a lot when I asked, in times of confusion during that year, "what would happen if I surrendered?"

What choosing a word does is to open up the year before you. It gives you something to explore, to look forward to and pay attention to as the weeks roll by. Sometimes you'll forget your word and need to be reminded. But it's working on you nonetheless, whether you pay careful attention or not. You're in a relationship with it that will unfold, as opposed to a resolution, which is more of a chore to be done: it's a finite idea with no room for movement, it chides you.

Once you and your word have found each other,
it's good to look up the derivation in a respectable
dictionary and learn its origins. *Cherish* is the
word that claimed me this week — a 14th century
word with tri-fold roots in the Latin "carus,"
which means "dear," the Old Irish "carae," or
friend, and the Sanskrit "kama," love. I also like
its definitions of "nurture," and "to harbor in the
mind deeply and resolutely."

Usually what I discover from my word isn't
something I ever could have predicted. Try it, and
see what happens to you.

Contrails & Happiness

Don't tell anyone, but I have a secret. I've been keeping it quiet — this is mid-January, people are cold and cranky and everyone I know seems to be arguing, either in person or on Facebook — I haven't wanted to irritate anyone further.

Most of the arguments — incredibly heated, the kind that wreck friendships in the blink of an eye — are about things like whether contrails are a natural result of airplane flight or a government plan to change our atmosphere. Or how long we have until global warming kills us off: six years? 25 years? Can we reverse the effects? Is global warming a liberal fantasy in the first place?

I know how an argument like this — big question, impossible to answer — can jeopardize an otherwise thriving relationship. My favorite ex-boyfriend Tad and I only had one subject we truly, passionately, disagreed on: whether O.J. Simpson was innocent. From here it seems ridiculous, but we almost came to blows. Once a year this would come up and ruin a day for us. We never resolved it: neither capitulated to the other's view. We either got tired of fighting or something else struck us as funny and once we got laughing together again, we were fine. Tad is dead now, so I've won the argument by default, which is no consolation.

In my humble opinion, arguments over O.J., contrails, and global warming are part of a basic issue that everyone faces: are we in control of our lives, or are we powerless? And if we're powerless, how can we learn to bear it?

Not being in control is a primal human fear. Without agency, how will we survive? We try to protect ourselves with knowledge, skills, understanding, or surrender. Yet even those who've turned themselves over to one of the gods and said "Thy will be done." still get plenty attached to the placement of a backyard fence.

Powerlessness is something we run into all the time. Sudden death from disease or car crash. Betrayal, adultery, divorce, the roulette wheel landing on red instead of black. Genetics. Admitting this — carrying it around in your breast pocket every day, is hard. But not admitting it keeps you constantly battle-ready, likely to join every argument-du-jour just to prove to yourself and others that you're in charge.

You're not in charge. Neither am I. That's no secret.

My secret is that ever since October 9th, the day I suddenly accepted that I had been powerless when I was being hurt as a kid — which happened in a fancy restaurant in Portland, Oregon of all places, and felt entirely physical, like being doused with ice water — I've been slowly growing happier and happier.

It's January. I'm still single. Wrinkles still crowd onto my face like shipwreck-survivors into a lifeboat. My bank account, as usual, nestles comfortably in the low three figures. The weather's unseasonably warm and white lines crisscross the winter sky. Nothing in my life has changed.

Except I'm happy. So everything's changed.

Notes

p. 99: "Stockholm Syndrome" has been included in the human resource guidelines of the International Brotherhood of Electrical Workers, Local 111.

p. 119: The line of poetry is from "The Lyre" by Dorianne Laux, *ORION Magazine*, September/October, 2010 issue.

Acknowledgements

Where shall I start? Anne Lamott was my first writing teacher, Dorianne Laux was my poetry teacher, Adair Lara taught me crucial things about personal essays, Margot Silk Forrest taught me to edit and suffer my work to be edited, Steve Baker and Melissa Thomas taught me to talk on the radio, Carolyn Crane gave me the scary dream job of writing commentary on any subject I chose, and Mike Thornton, Brian Bahouth, Paul Emery, Brian Terhorst, and David Levin let me keep doing it. Christine Bonner allowed me to use her gorgeous harp music as my intro. Sarah Fisk gave me important advice in the nick of time. Nancy Shanteau kept me going through the rough spots. The job itself taught me to meet a weekly deadline, record in one take, and turn sentences inside out in order to cram them into three minutes. Copious on-going love and thanks to them all!

For support and encouragement, many many many thanks to Ellen Aisenbrey, Peggy Bean, Jacquie Bellon, Jane Bradley, Julie Bradley, Judy Crowe, Kate Dwyer, Paula Elliott, Gail & Charles Entrekin, Dawn Fischer, Sam Fisk, Ruth Ghio, Mikail Graham, Kathy Gronau, Oakley Hall, III, Robert Lee Haycock, Amanda Hobart, Elaine James, Maxima Kahn, Lois Karpenko, Julia Kelliher, Ellen Kelman, Marilyn Kriegel, Anita Montero, Sari Oseasohn, Utah Phillips, Hilary Putnam, Judie Rae, Diane Robertson, Joanna Robinson, Briana Rose, Steve Sanfield, Eileen Schmitz, Stevie & Bill Sheatsley, Louie Sheridan, Skip Alan Smith, Sarah Sparks, Jinny St. Goar, Catherine Stifter, Jane Swan, Uncle John, Jerianne Van Dijk, Maya Vasquez, Susanna Wilson, Judy Work, the Community of Writers at Squaw Valley, Sierra Mountain Coffee Roasters, Sierra Nevada Memorial Hospital's Cancer Center, and everyone who listens on KVMR.

And big love to the generous and game Kickstarter supporters I haven't already thanked above: Lori Alaways, Deanna Allen, Ana Athanasiu, Susan Bartoletti, Ruth Bavetta, Leah Bird, Padee Black, Deanie Blank, Rebecca Bowler, Nancy

Braymiller, Roseanne Burke, James Ian Burns, Katie Carter, Shaun Case, Jen Castle, Catharine Clark-Sayles, Caroline Courtright, Susan Crocenzi, Chris Hancock Donaldson, Lori Gay, Jim Golden, Lynn Goodwin, Lisa Greer, Heidi Hall, Sarah Heick, Shawna Hein, Jan Hersh, Talei Hoblitzell, Catherine Abbey Hodges, Christine Irving, Carol Ann Johnston, Frances Jorgensen, Cristine Kelly, Lakin Khan, Georg Kickinger, Bob Kriegel, Jeannene Langford, Melissa Latimer, Gail Carson Levine, Irene Lipshin, Andrea Livingston, Terry Lowe, Moira Magneson, Fred Marchant, Dawn McDuffie, Shanda McGrew, Dawn McGuire, Paul McShane, Margo Meredith, Larry Miller, Erin Murphy, Susan Nance, Nancy Nelson, Karen Neuberg, Elisa Parker, Mary Peterson, Sarah Putnam, Barbara Ras, Erica Randall, Amanda Rogers, Lilith Rogers, Cathy Roos, Patti Sarkisian, Katherine Shad, Naima Shea, Terry Shearn, Elaine Sierra, Bren Smith, Margaret Stawowy, John Taber, Ginger Thomson, Julie Torres, Dennis Trujillo, Douglass Truth, Carolee Whitman, Homer Wills, Marjorie Woodall, Laurie Woodum, Kathy Wronski, and Scott Young. Your support during that campaign is what made this book possible.

About the Author

Poet Molly Fisk writes weekly essays for community radio stations in California, Colorado, Illinois and Wisconsin. She's the author of the poetry collections, *The More Difficult Beauty, Listening to Winter,* and *Salt Water Poems,* and the audio recordings of commentary, *Blow-Drying a Chicken* and *Using Your Turn Signal Promotes World Peace.* Fisk has been awarded grants by the National Endowment for the Arts, the California Arts Council, and the Corporation for Public Broadcasting. She's the owner of Poetry Boot Camp (poetrybootcamp.com) and can be reached at mollyfisk.com.

CPSIA information can be obtained
at www.ICGtesting.com
Printed in the USA
FSHW021247210220
67392FS

9 780989 495806